TWELVE TRIBES OF ISRAEL

Activity Book for Beginners

DEFENDERS OF THE FAITH

Twelve Tribes of Israel Activity Book for Beginners

Bible Pathway Adventures® is a trademark of BPA Publishing Ltd.
Defenders of the Faith® is a trademark of BPA Publishing Ltd.

ISBN: 978-1-989961-72-8

Author: Pip Reid

Creative Director: Curtis Reid

For free Bible resources including coloring pages, worksheets, puzzles and more, visit our website at:

shop.biblepathwayadventures.com

 # Introduction for Parents

Enjoy teaching your children about the ancient Israelites with our *Twelve Tribes of Israel Activity Book for Beginners*. From Jacob (Israel) and his sons in Canaan to the Israelites entry into the Promised Land, children will LOVE learning the history of the twelve tribes of Israel. Packed with fun worksheets, coloring pages, and puzzles to help educators just like you teach young ones the Biblical faith.

Bible Pathway Adventures® helps educators teach children the Biblical faith in a fun and engaging way. We do this via our Activity Books and free printable activities – available on our website: www.biblepathwayadventures.com

Thanks for buying this Activity Book and supporting our ministry. Every book purchased helps us continue our work providing free Classroom Packs and discipleship resources to families and missions everywhere.

The search for Truth is more fun than Tradition!

Table of Contents

Crafts & Projects

I am an Israelite

Twelve tribes of Israel

A long time ago in the land of Canaan, there lived a Hebrew man named Jacob. He had four wives: Leah and Rachel (who were his real wives), and Bilhah and Zilpah (who were his concubines). Together they had twelve sons; Reuben, Simeon, Levi, Judah, Dan, Naphtali, Gad, Asher, Issachar, Zebulun, Joseph, and Benjamin. The descendants of these twelve sons became the twelve tribes of Israel (Genesis 49).

Each tribe was named after a son or grandson of Jacob (Israel). Even though the tribes became one nation, each tribe was very different. In fact, they were so different that Jacob gave each son a different blessing before he died.

Many years later, after the Hebrews had lived in slavery in Egypt, Yah used a man named Moses to bring them out of Egypt and into the land of Canaan, the Promised Land. Along the way, the Hebrews became the great nation of Israel. And they had many adventures. Let's become Torah time-travelers and learn about the twelve tribes of Israel!

Did You Know?

Yah changed Jacob's name to Israel after he fought an angel of Yah (Genesis 32:28). Israel means, "to wrestle with Yah and men, and overcome."

ASHER

DAN

GAD

ZEBULUN

⊱ J is for Jacob ⊰

Jacob was the son of Isaac and grandson of Abraham.
The 12 tribes of Israel were named after Jacob's sons
and grandsons. Trace the letters. Color the picture.

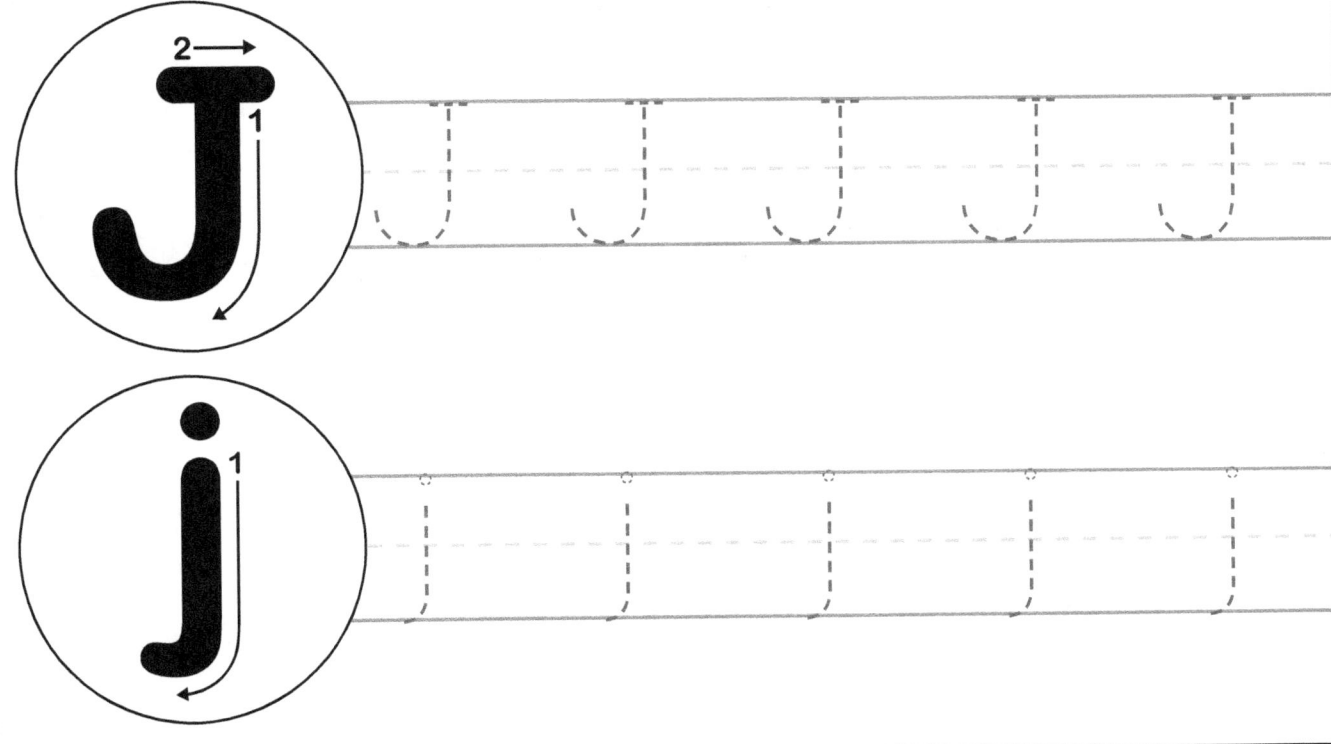

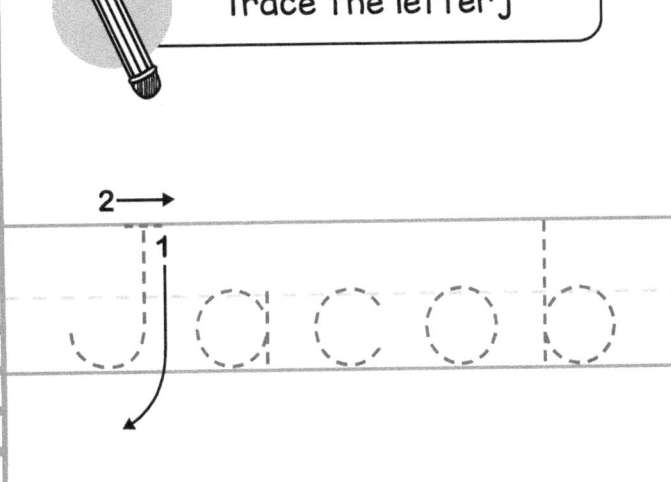

Trace the letter j

Color Jacob

Jacob's new name

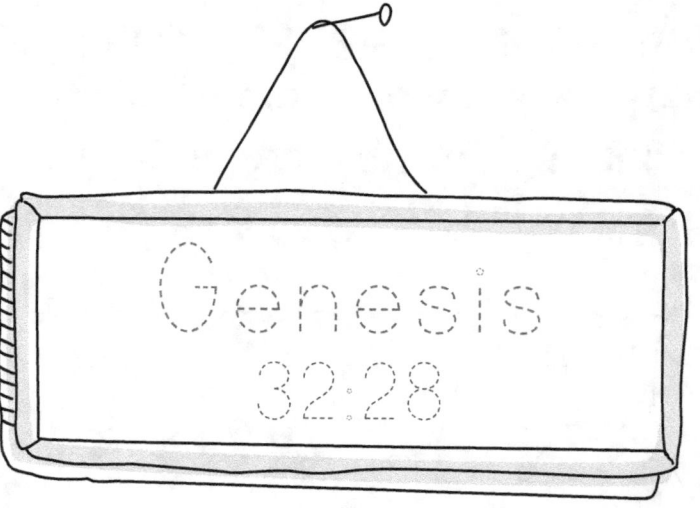

Genesis
32:28

Your name will

not be Jacob.

It will be Israel.

The family of Jacob (Israel)

Jacob had two wives and two concubines.
Their names were Leah, Rachel, Zilpah, and Bilhah.
How many sons did they have? Count the sons
and write the number in the box.

Leah
My sons are Reuben,
Simeon, Levi, Judah,
Issachar, Zebulun

Rachel
My sons are Joseph,
Benjamin

Zilpah
(Leah's maid)
My sons are Gad,
Asher

Bilhah
(Rachel's maid)
My sons are Dan,
Naphtali

Twelve sons of Jacob (Israel)

Jacob had twelve sons. Who were they?
Write a name below each box. Color the pictures.

Twelve sons of Jacob (Israel)

Trace the names. Color the pictures.

Reuben

Simeon

Levi

Judah

Dan

Naphtali

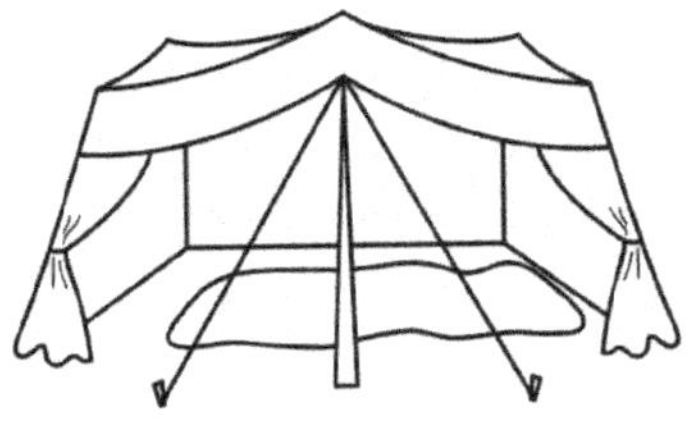

Gad

Asher

Issachar

Zebulun

Joseph

Benjamin

Sheep and goats

Jacob and his sons lived in the land of Canaan.
They were shepherds. They took care of the sheep
and goats. Color the sheep yellow. Color the goats blue.

🌿 To Egypt... 🌿

Joseph was one of Jacob's twelve sons.
They sold him to traders for 20 pieces of silver.
The traders took him to the land of Egypt (Genesis 37:18-28).
Connect the dots to show Joseph's journey.

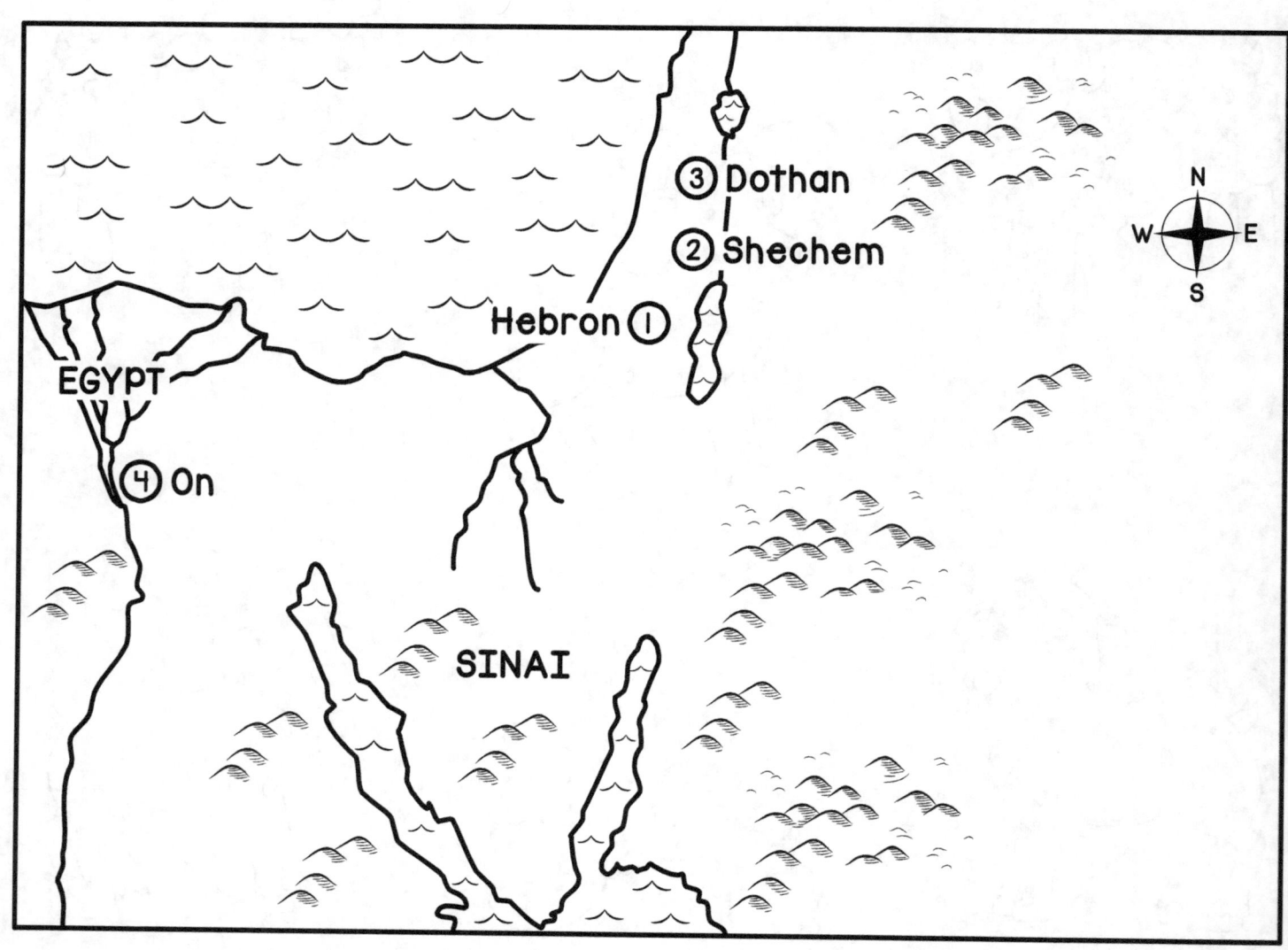

🌿 Pieces of silver 🌿

Jacob's sons sold Joseph to the traders
for 20 pieces of silver. The traders took Joseph
to the land of Egypt.

Design your own piece of silver in the space below.

Potiphar is blessed!

In Egypt, Joseph worked hard for a man named Potiphar.
He made Joseph ruler over his house (Genesis 39:1-6).
Color Potiphar's house.

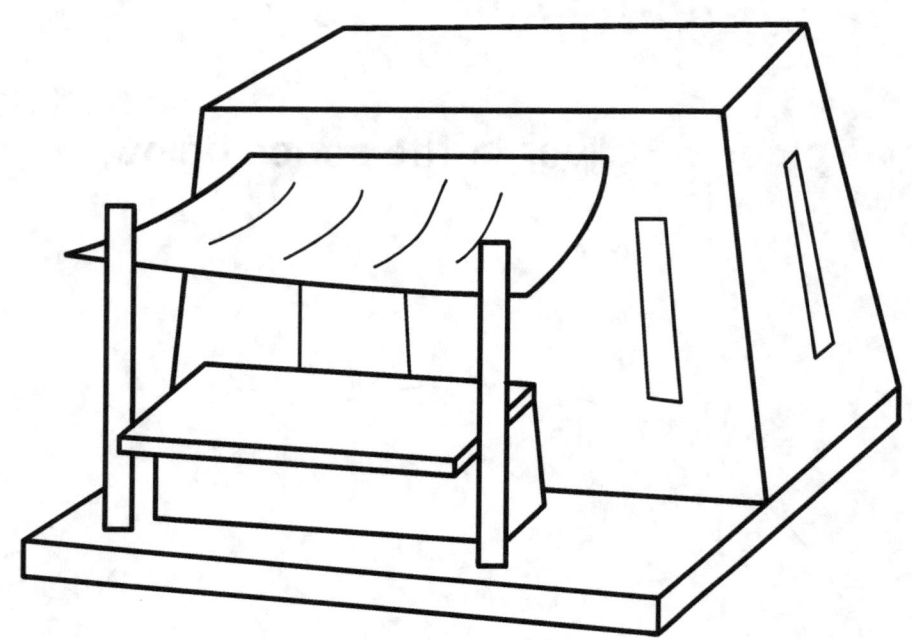

Yah blessed everything in Potiphar's house and
fields because of Joseph. Color the house objects
RED. Color the field objects BROWN.

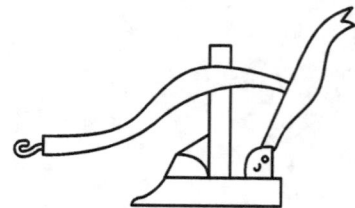

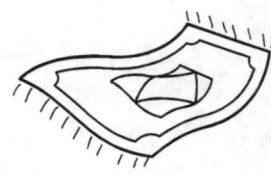

 # Joseph explains two dreams

Potiphar's wife told lies about Joseph, so Potiphar
threw him in prison. There Joseph met a butler
and a baker. The butler dreamed about grapes.
The baker dreamed about bread. Joseph helped
them understand their dreams (Genesis 40:1-19).
Match the dream with the prisoner.

butler

"Pharaoh will cut off
your head and hang
you from a tree."

baker

"Pharaoh will let you
go back to work."

Joseph's chariot

While Joseph was in prison, he helped Pharaoh understand his two dreams. Pharaoh was happy! He made Joseph a ruler of Egypt and told him to ride in a special chariot (Genesis 41:41-43). Draw Joseph inside the chariot.

I spy!

Joseph saved food in Egypt for seven years. He stored the food in the cities (Genesis 41:48). What food did he save? Color the same food a single color. Then count each type of food and write the number on the label.

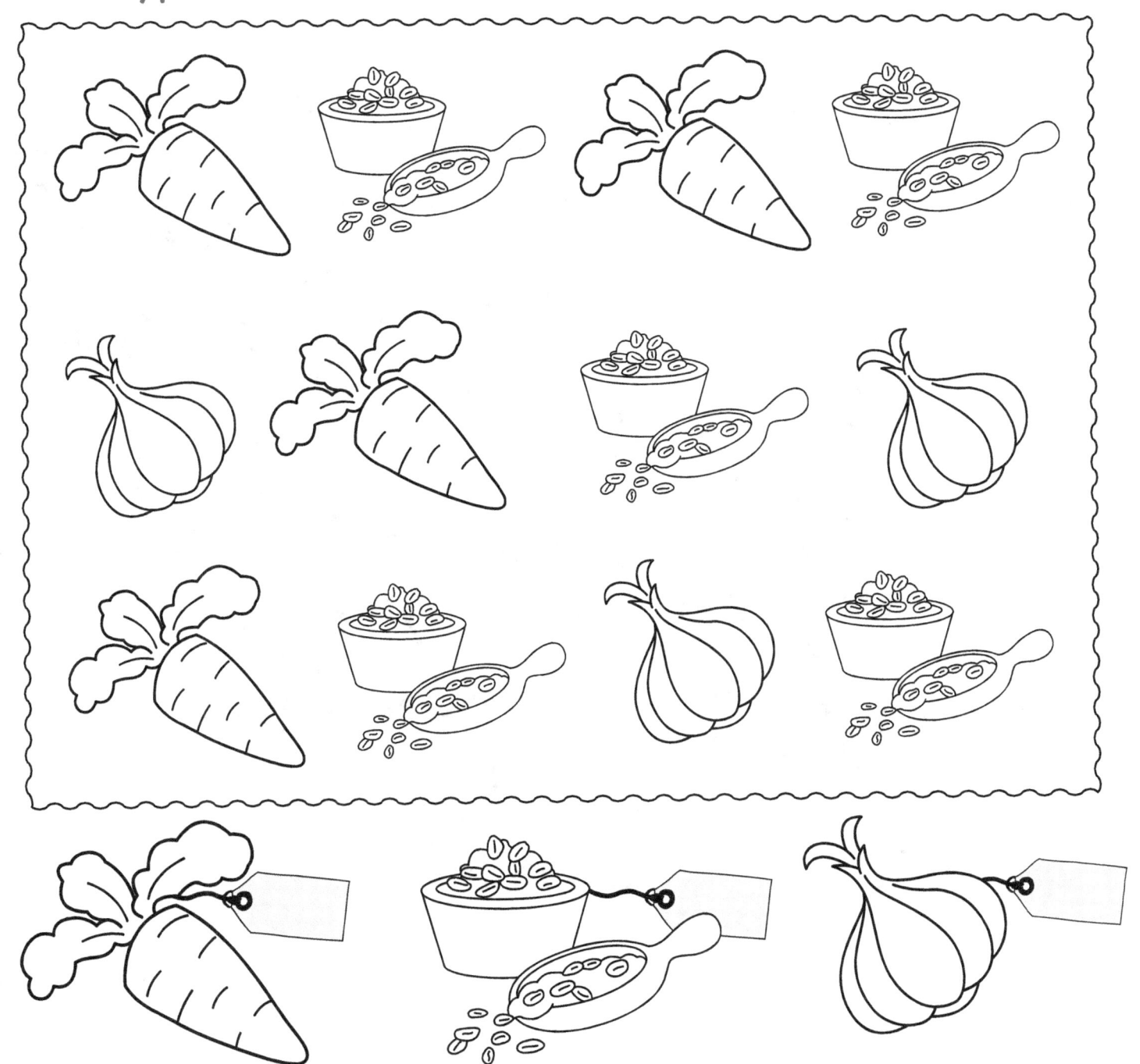

🌿 Famine in Canaan 🌿

Jacob and his sons didn't have enough food to eat.
Help Jacob's sons get to the land of Egypt to buy food.

Joseph helps his brothers

Read Genesis 42:25. When Joseph saw his brothers, he wanted to help them. What items did he give them to take home? Trace a dotted line from each item to the donkey. Color the pictures.

🌿 The silver cup 🌿

After some time, the brothers came back to Egypt. Joseph told a servant to hide his silver cup in Benjamin's sack. Connect the dots to see the picture.

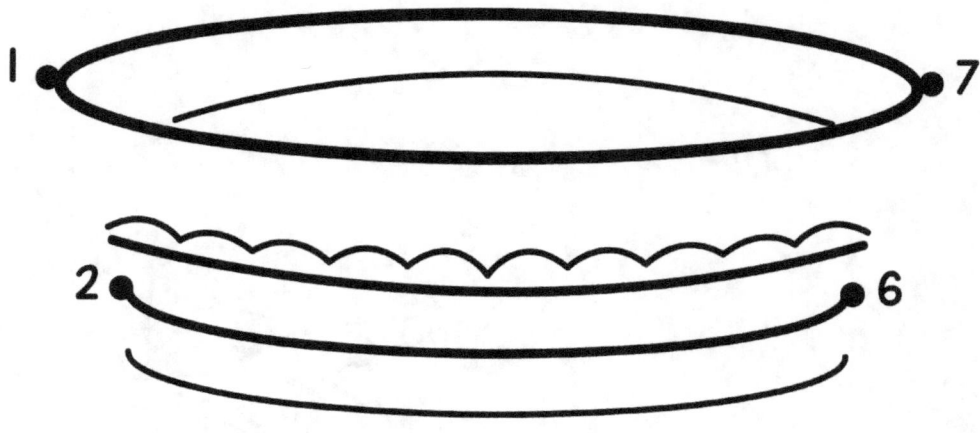

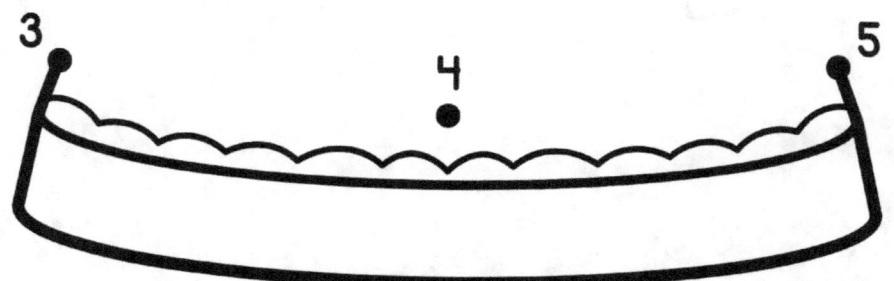

Joseph's secret

Fill in the blanks using the chart below. What do you see?

What did Joseph tell his brothers?

____ ____ ____
 9   1   13

____ ____ ____ ____
 25   15   21   18

____ ____ ____ ____ ____ ____ ____
 2   18   15   20   8   5   18

A	B	C	D	E	F	G	H	I	J	K	L	M
1	2	3	4	5	6	7	8	9	10	11	12	13

N	O	P	Q	R	S	T	U	V	W	X	Y	Z
14	15	16	17	18	19	20	21	22	23	24	25	26

🌿 Surprise! 🌿

Read Genesis 45:1-3. Joseph told his brothers who he was.
How did his brothers feel? Draw their faces below.

F is for forgive

Joseph knew God had planned everything from the beginning.
He forgave his brothers for selling him into slavery.
Now Jacob's twelve sons were together again!
Trace the words. Color the picture.

F is for forgive

Israel goes to Egypt

Joseph's family came to the land of Egypt to live near Joseph. They used wagons to bring their goods and animals with them (Genesis 45:21-46:5). Trace the circles.

Land of Egypt

Israel and his family lived in the land of Egypt for many years. Find and circle each of the words from the list below.

```
D D D N G S
L A N D O O
E R T M D N
E G Y P T S
I S R A E L
J O S E P H
```

EGYPT   GOD
SONS   LAND
ISRAEL   JOSEPH

Where is Egypt?

The Hebrews lived in the land of Egypt for many years.
Color Egypt green. Color the water blue.

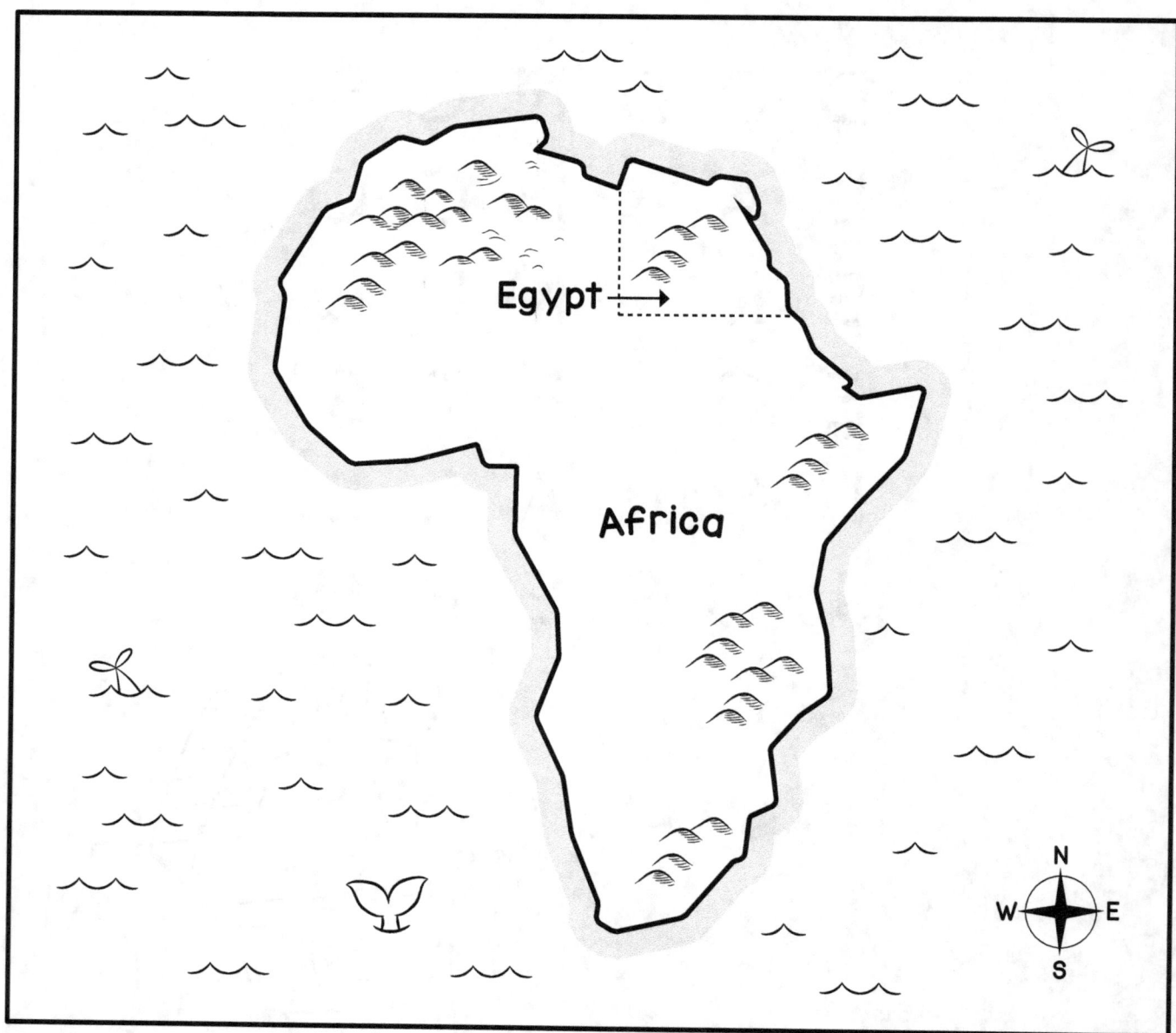

Slaves in Egypt

The Hebrews had many children.
Egypt was full of Hebrews! Pharaoh was scared.
He made them work harder and harder
until they asked Yah to save them.

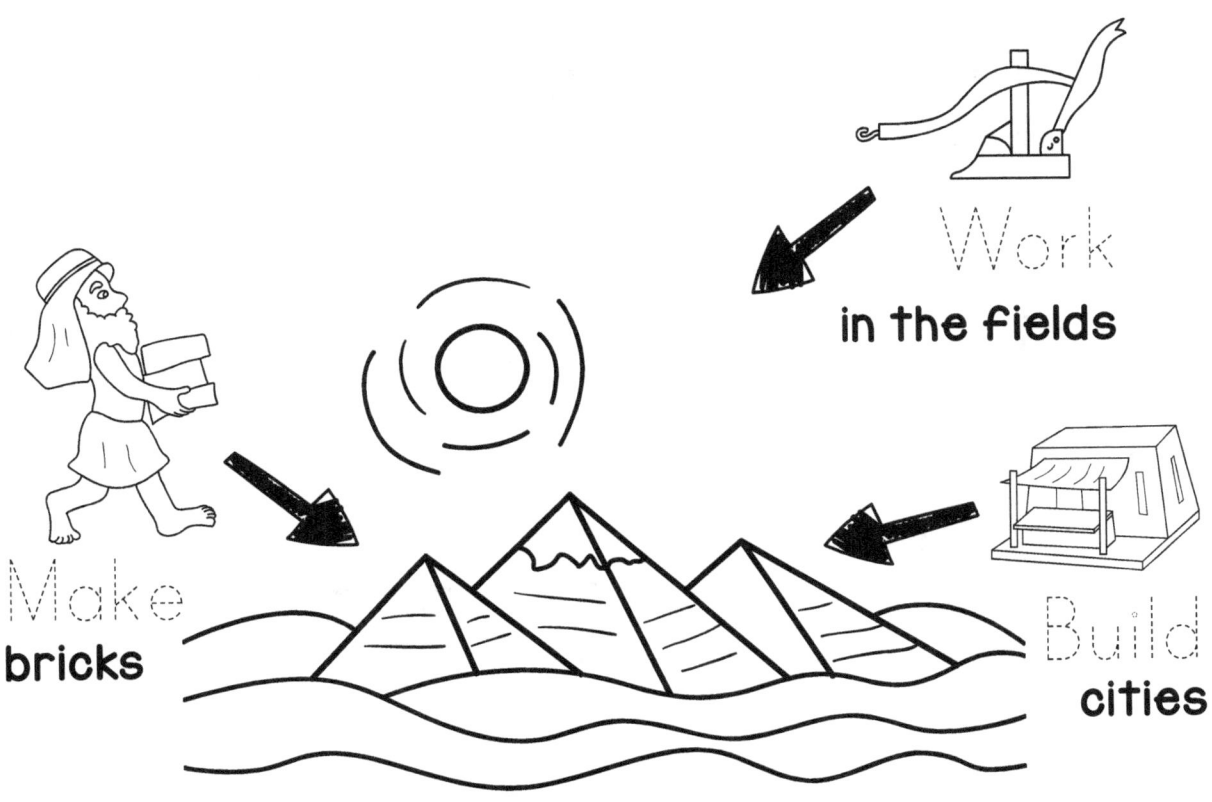

Work
in the fields

Make
bricks

Build
cities

I See a Hebrew

🌿 Who was Moses? 🌿

Fill in the blanks using the chart below. What do you see?

Who was
Moses?

___ ___ ___ ___ ___
13 15 19 5 19

___ ___ ___   ___
23 1 19   1

___ ___ ___ ___ ___ ___
8 5 2 18 5 23

A	B	C	D	E	F	G	H	I	J	K	L	M
1	2	3	4	5	6	7	8	9	10	11	12	13

N	O	P	Q	R	S	T	U	V	W	X	Y	Z
14	15	16	17	18	19	20	21	22	23	24	25	26

Yah's plan for
Moses

Moses was born in   Egypt.

He was a Hebrew.

Moses ran away to   Midian

Yah told him, "Free My people."

Moses went back to Egypt.

He asked   Pharaoh

to free the Hebrews.

The king of Egypt

Pharaoh was the king of Egypt.
Moses and Aaron asked him to let the Hebrews go
(Exodus 7:10). Trace the words. Color the picture.

The king of Egypt

Moses and Aaron before Pharaoh

Aaron obeyed God's instructions.
He threw down his staff before Pharaoh and
it became a snake. Can you follow instructions
like Aaron? Use the color code to finish the picture.

1 = green	2 = red	3 = yellow	4 = brown

www.biblepathwayadventures.com
Twelve Tribes of Israel (Beginners)

© BPA Publishing Ltd 2022

🌿 The ten plagues 🌿

Yah wanted to free the Israelites. He sent ten plagues on Egypt. Can you count them and write the number?

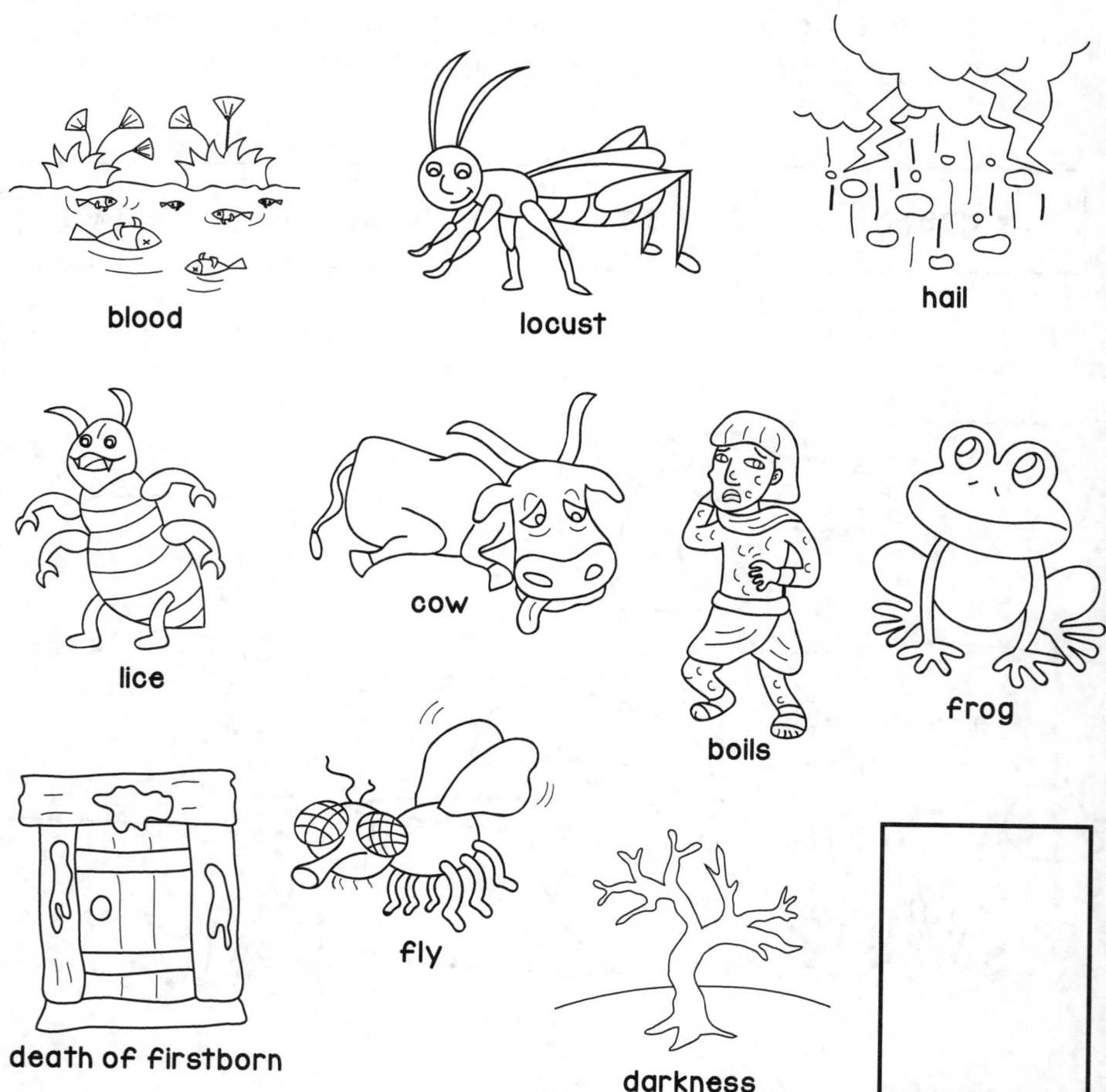

blood

locust

hail

lice

cow

boils

frog

death of firstborn

fly

darkness

🍃 The Passover 🍃

The 10th plague was the death of the firstborn. Yah protected the Israelites from this plague. He told them to put lamb's blood on the top and sides of their doorways (Exodus 12). Draw blood on the top and sides of the door.

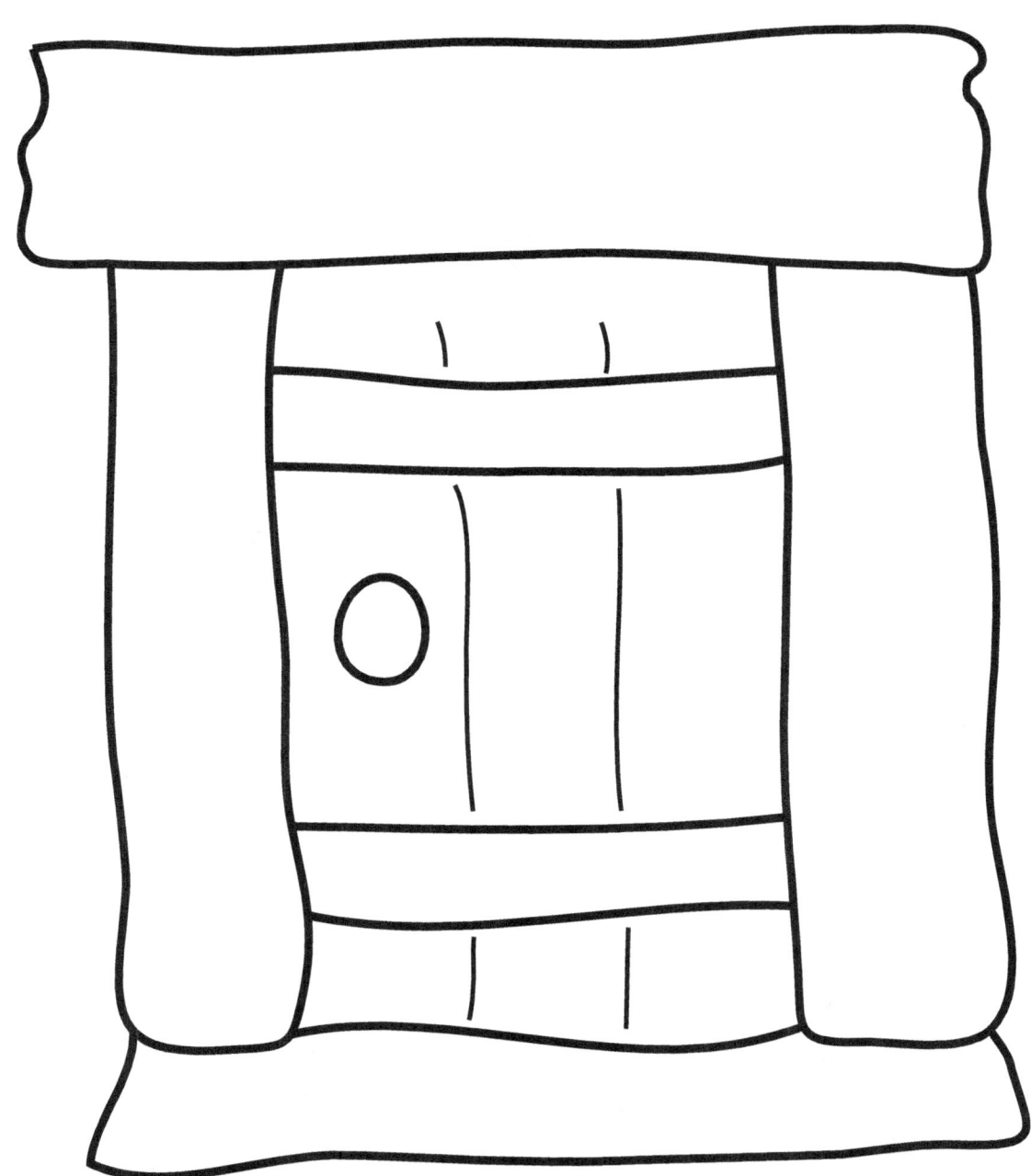

The Passover Meal

The Israelites ate lamb, bitter herbs, and bread without yeast (matzah) at the first Passover meal. Draw the food you eat for the Passover.

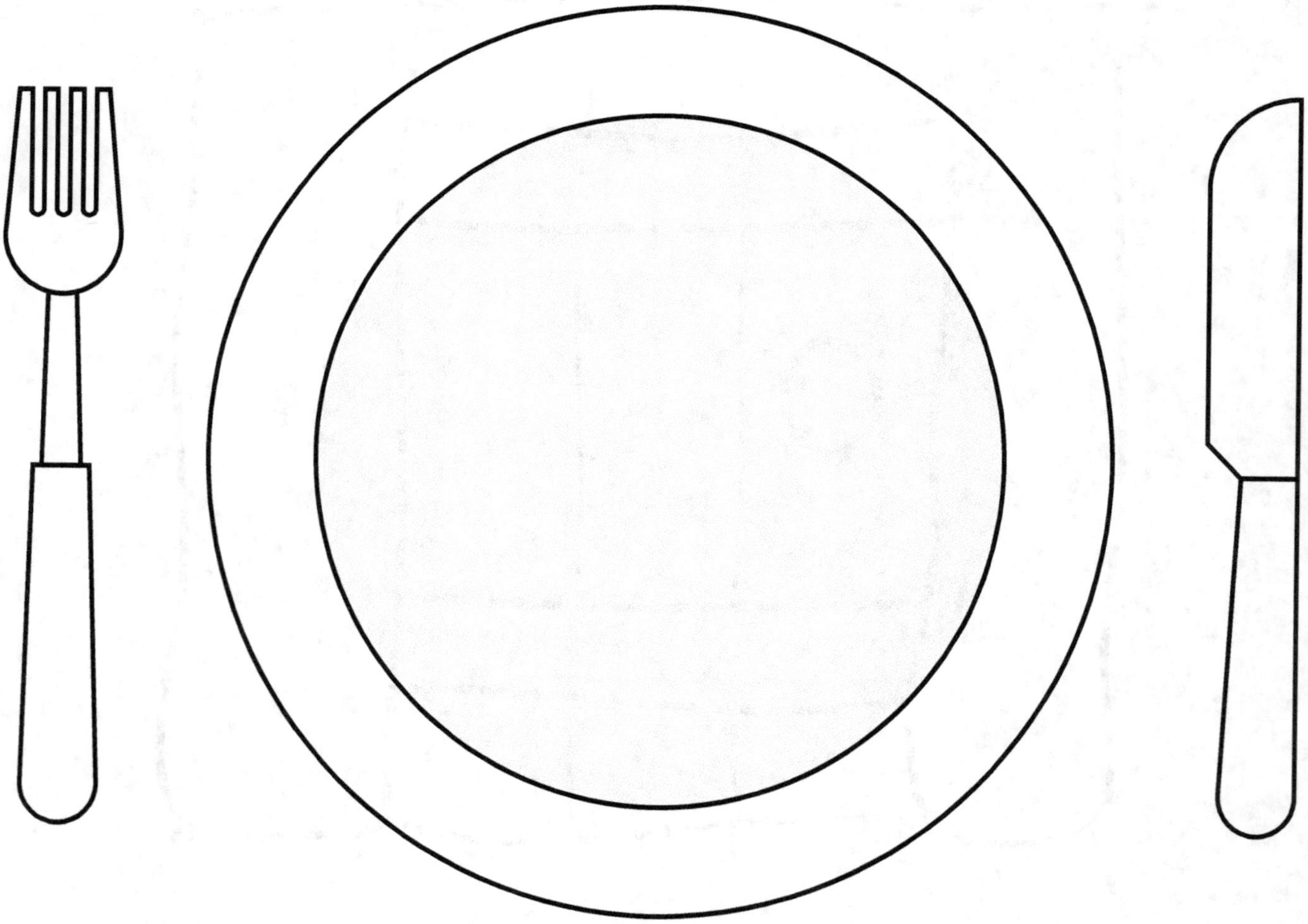

✦ Matzah ✦

The Hebrew word for unleavened bread is matzah. Matzah is a type of bread made with flour and water. The Israelites left Egypt during the Feast of Unleavened Bread (Exodus 13). In the box below, draw a piece of matzah for each person in your family. How many pieces of matzah did you draw?

matzah

מַצָּה

Unleavened bread

🌿 Let's Go! 🌿

If I had to leave Egypt, I would take these items with me...

....

....

....

....

Help the Israelites cross the Red Sea

Educators: Read Exodus 14. Ask children questions about crossing the Red Sea. When they answer correctly, they can color a square and move through the sea until they reach the other side.

🌿 Manna and quail 🌿

Yah took care of the Israelites in the wilderness.
Every day, He sent them manna and quail to eat
(Exodus 16). Color the food He sent in the morning RED.
Color the food He sent in the evening BLUE.

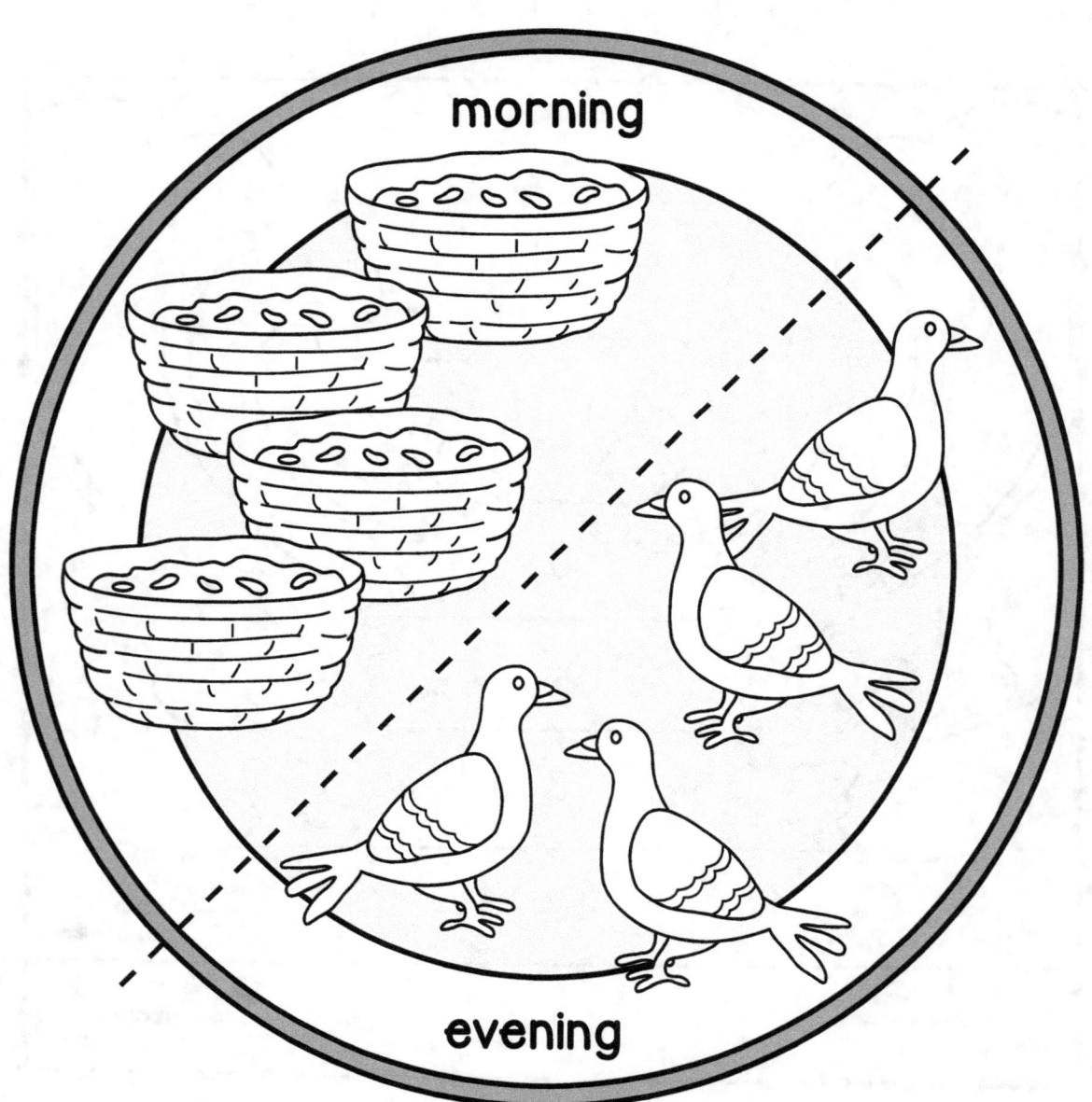

Water from the rock

Yah gave the Israelites water to drink from a rock (Exodus 17). Glue pieces of blue paper onto the rock to make a waterfall!

Israel at Mount Sinai

The Israelites camped at Mount Sinai. A thick cloud came down onto the mountain. There was thunder and lightning and a loud sound from a shofar. (Exodus 19:16) Trace the cloud and lightning bolts. Color the picture.

🌿 Mount Sinai 🌿

Find and circle each of the words from the list below.

```
T  E  N  G  T  C
S  T  A  O  E  A
X  W  W  D  N  M
P  N  C  S  T  P
S  H  O  F  A  R
F  I  R  E  L  J
```

FIRE   **TENT**

TEN   **GOD**

SHOFAR   **CAMP**

The ten commandments

In the wilderness, Yah gave the Israelites
the ten commandments (Exodus 20:1-17).
Read the ten commandments. Color the pictures.

**I am Yah your
God. Do not have
other gods**

**Do not
make idols**

**Do not take
the name of God
in vain**

**Remember
the Sabbath**

**Honor your
father and mother**

Do not
murder

Do not commit
adultery

Do not
steal

Do not
lie

Do not want other
people's things

T is for tribe

A tribe is a big group of people. They are usually from the same family. There are twelve tribes of Israel. Trace the letters and word. Color the picture.

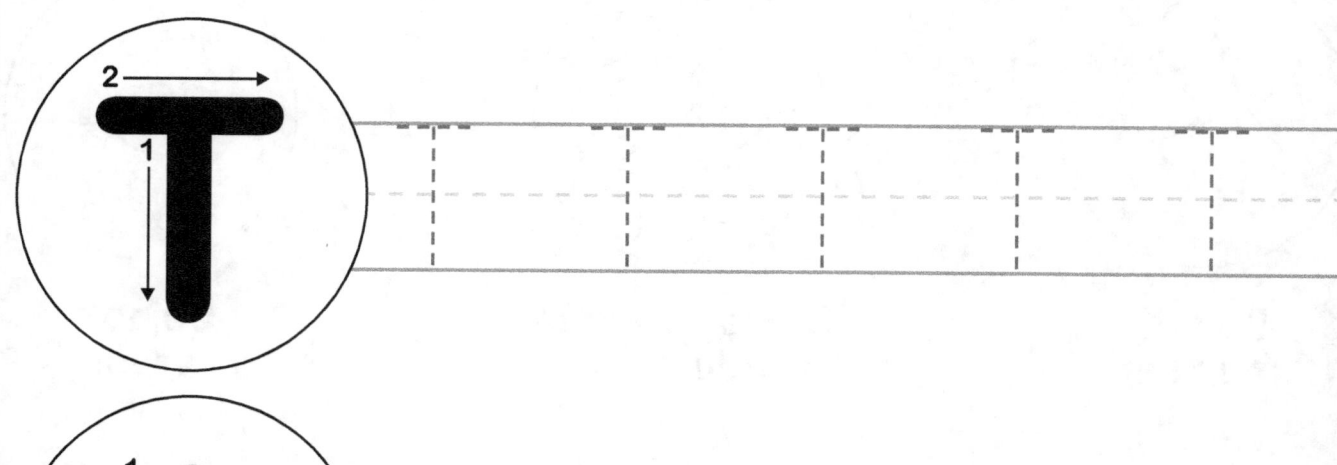

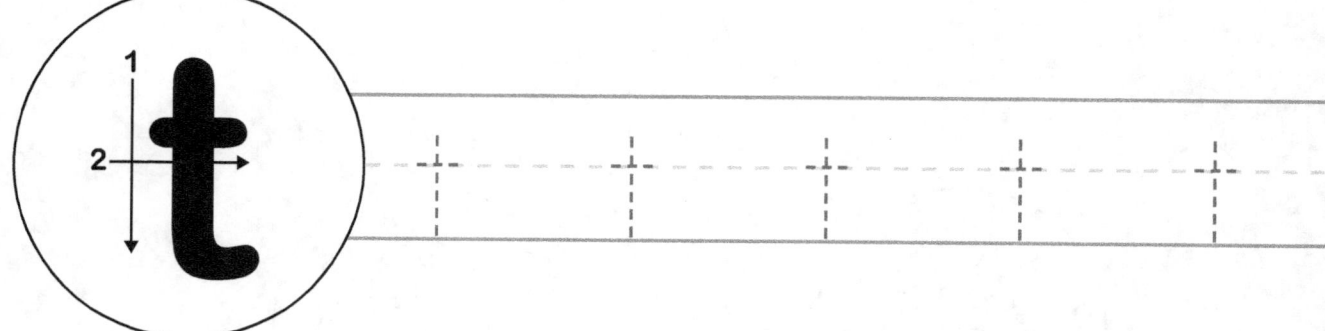

Trace the letter t

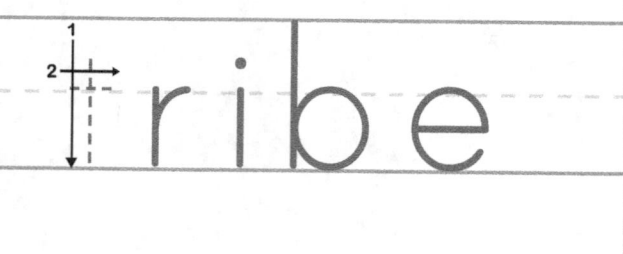

Color the banner.

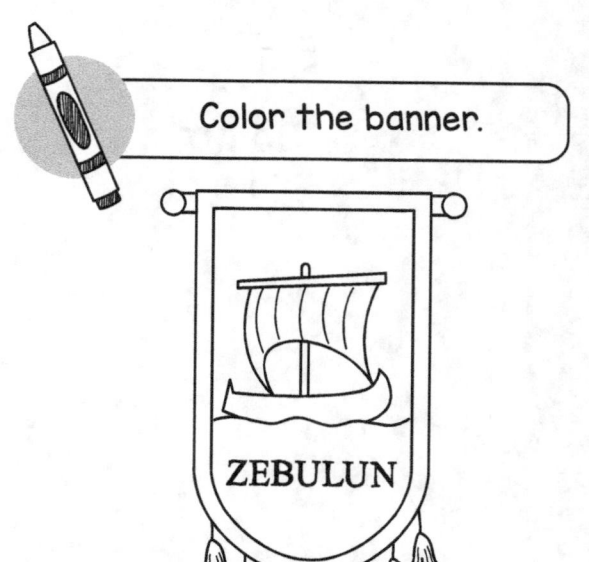

 Twelve tribes of Israel

The <u>descendants</u> of the 12 sons of Jacob (Israel) became the 12 tribes of Israel.

Sons

Reuben
Simeon
Levi
Judah
Dan
Naphtali
Gad
Asher
Issachar
Zebulun
Joseph
Benjamin

Tribes

Reuben
Simeon
~~Levi~~
Judah
Dan
Naphtali
Gad
Asher
Issachar
Zebulun
~~Joseph~~ Manasseh & Ephraim
Benjamin

Levi got no land but had to look after the tabernacle
Joseph was divided into two tribes: Manasseh & Ephraim

** <u>Descendants</u> are people born after the person in the same family.

🌿 Camp of Israel 🌿

In the wilderness, Yah told the Israelites to camp in a certain way. They camped in tribes on each side of the camp. Yah chose the tribe of Levi to serve as priests. They camped around the tabernacle.

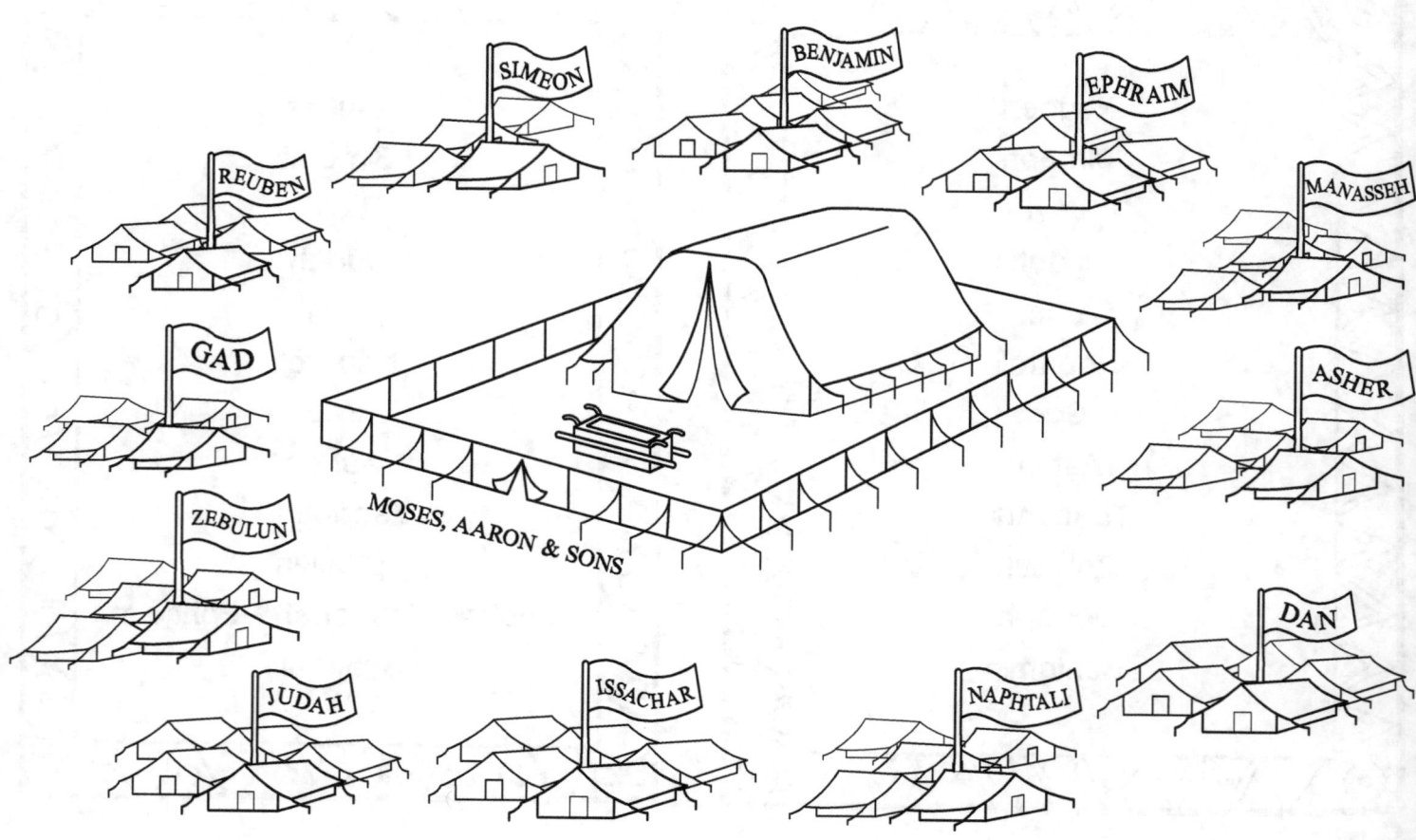

🌿 Twelve tribes of Israel 🌿

The twelve tribes of Israel in the wilderness (Numbers 1:1-47).

What's different?

Circle the picture that is different.

" This is Love for God: to obey His commandments. "

(I John 5:3)

❧ Tzitzits ❧

Yah asked the Israelites to wear tassels on their clothes (Numbers 15:38). This helped them remember the commandments. These tassels are called tzitzits.

Color and trace the set of tzitzits below.

🌿 The seventh day is.... 🌿

Fill in the blanks using the chart below.
What do you see?

What do you do on the Sabbath?

$$\overline{\quad}\ \overline{\quad}\ \overline{\quad}$$
20   8   5

$$\overline{\quad}\ \overline{\quad}\ \overline{\quad}\ \overline{\quad}\ \overline{\quad}\ \overline{\quad}\ \overline{\quad}$$
19   1   2   2   1   19   8

A	B	C	D	E	F	G	H	I	J	K	L	M
1	2	3	4	5	6	7	8	9	10	11	12	13

N	O	P	Q	R	S	T	U	V	W	X	Y	Z
14	15	16	17	18	19	20	21	22	23	24	25	26

 Seven

The Sabbath is on the 7th day.

Write the number seven in the boxes below.

How many fingers are there?

Read Exodus 20:11. What did Yah do on the 7th day?

....

The Appointed Times

In the wilderness, the Israelites learned about Yah's Feasts (Leviticus 23). He told them to celebrate these Feasts each year. These Feasts are also called 'The Appointed Times'.

Pesach + Chag HaMatzot

Bikkurim

Shavu'ot

Yom Teru'ah

Yom Kippur

Sukkot

Shemini Atzeret

The Spring Feasts

Chag HaMatzot, Bikkurim, and Shavu'ot take place in springtime. Yeshua fulfilled these Feasts. Trace and color the pictures.

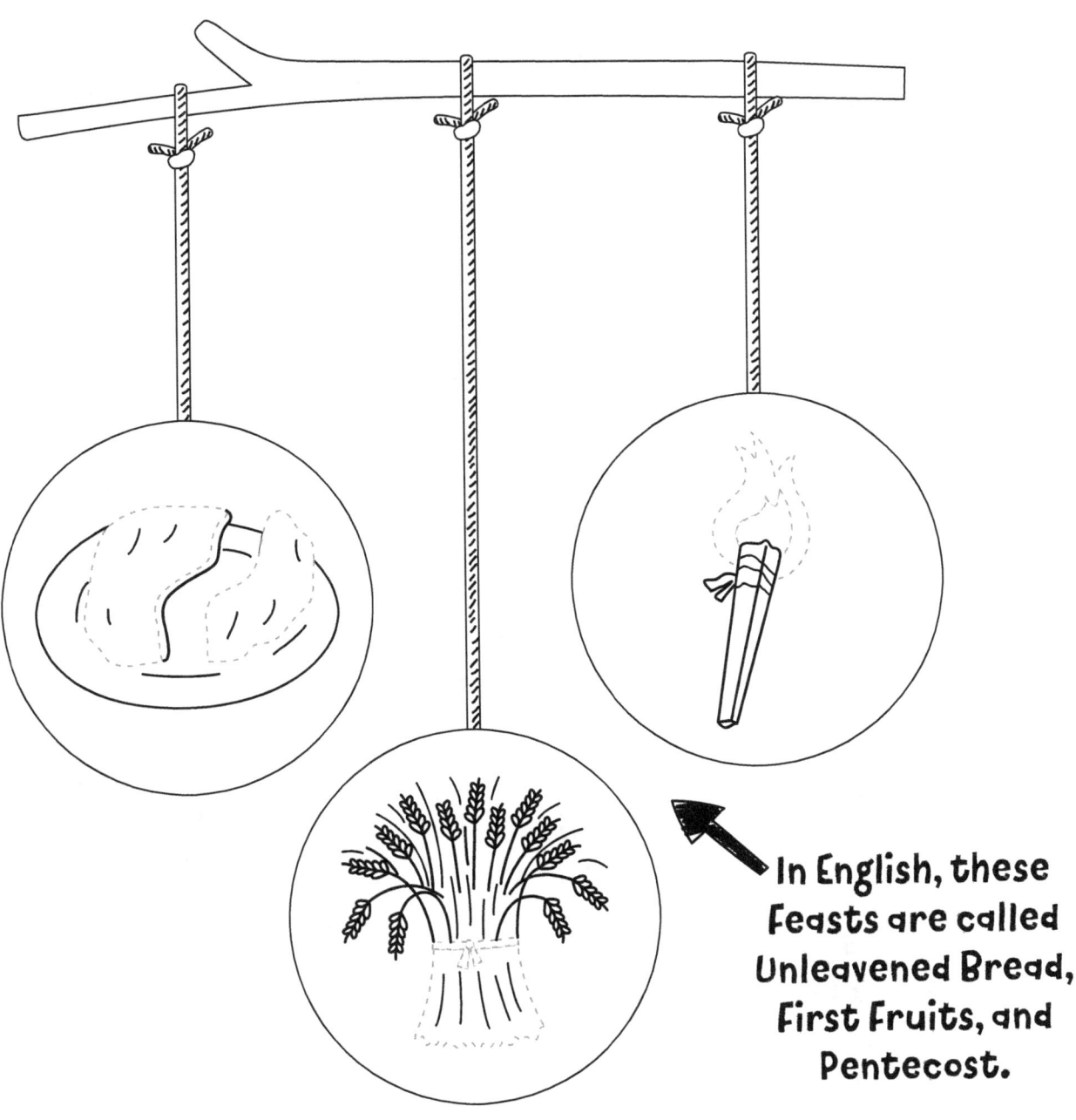

In English, these Feasts are called Unleavened Bread, First Fruits, and Pentecost.

The Fall Feasts

Yom Teru'ah, Yom Kippur, Sukkot and Shemini Atzeret take place in Fall. They all point to Yeshua.
Trace and color the pictures.

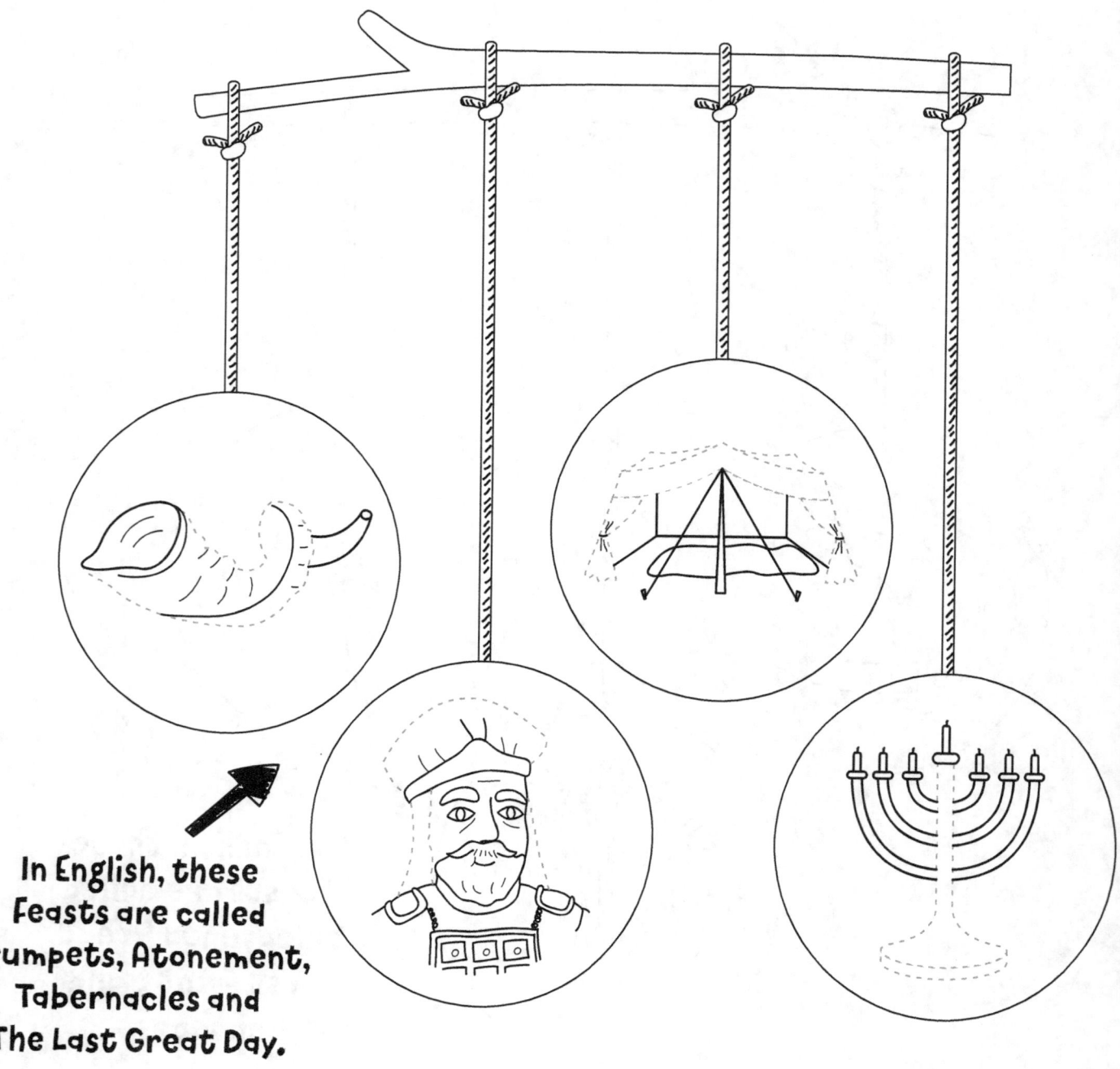

In English, these Feasts are called Trumpets, Atonement, Tabernacles and The Last Great Day.

DECORATE THE Sukkah

Tabernacle treasures

The Israelites built a tent (a tabernacle) in the desert to worship Yah. Inside they put special furniture items. Trace a dotted line from each item to the tabernacle. Color the pictures.

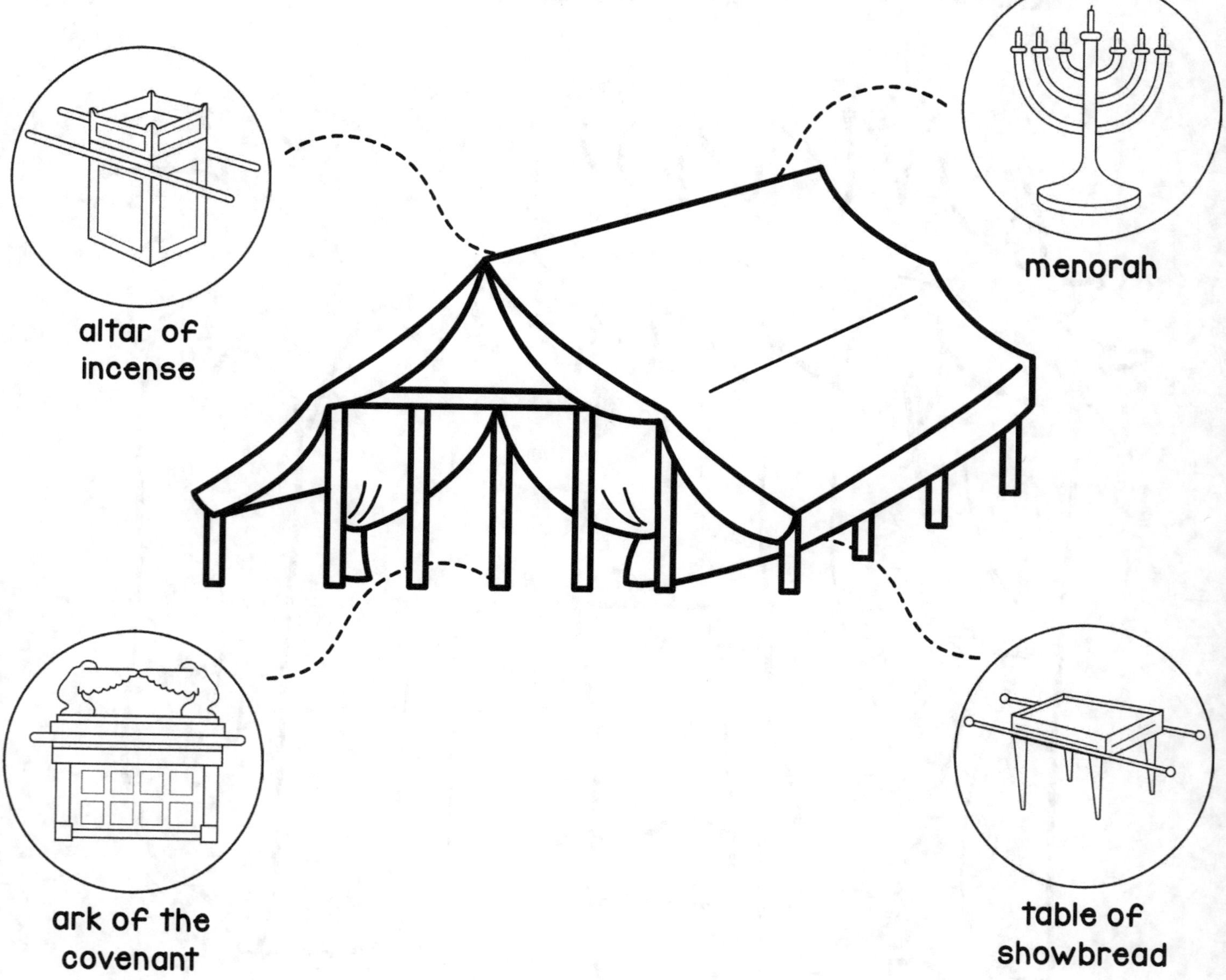

menorah

altar of
incense

ark of the
covenant

table of
showbread

🌿 Duties of a priest 🌿

The priests were of the tribe of Levi.
On the way to the Promised Land, Yah gave
them many jobs. Can you name them?
Trace the words. Color the pictures.

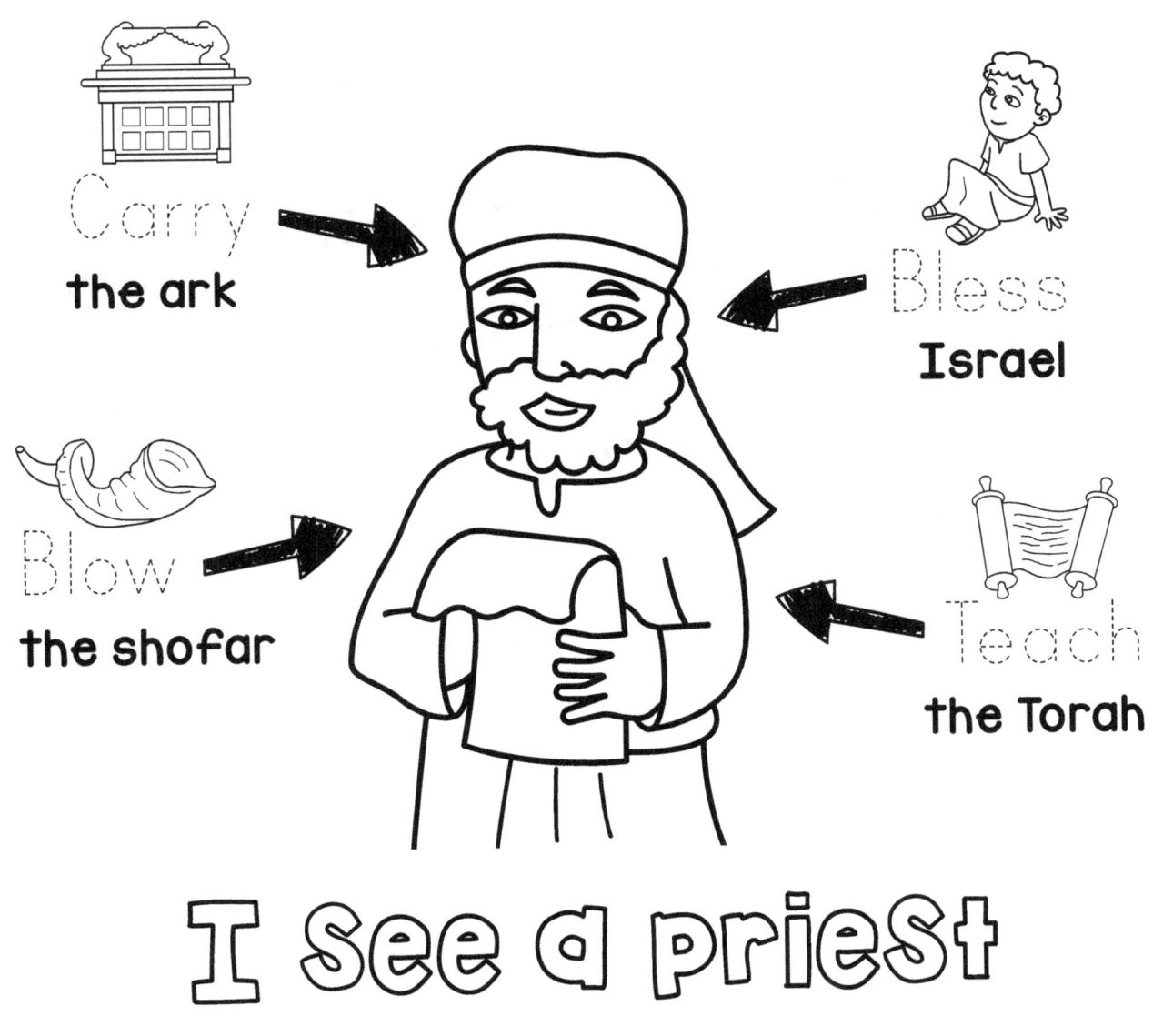

Carry
the ark

Blow
the shofar

Bless
Israel

Teach
the Torah

I see a priest

🌿 Ark of the covenant 🌿

The Israelite priests had a special job; to carry the ark of
the covenant. The ark was a box covered in gold.
The ten commandments were inside the ark.
Trace the squares. Color the ark.

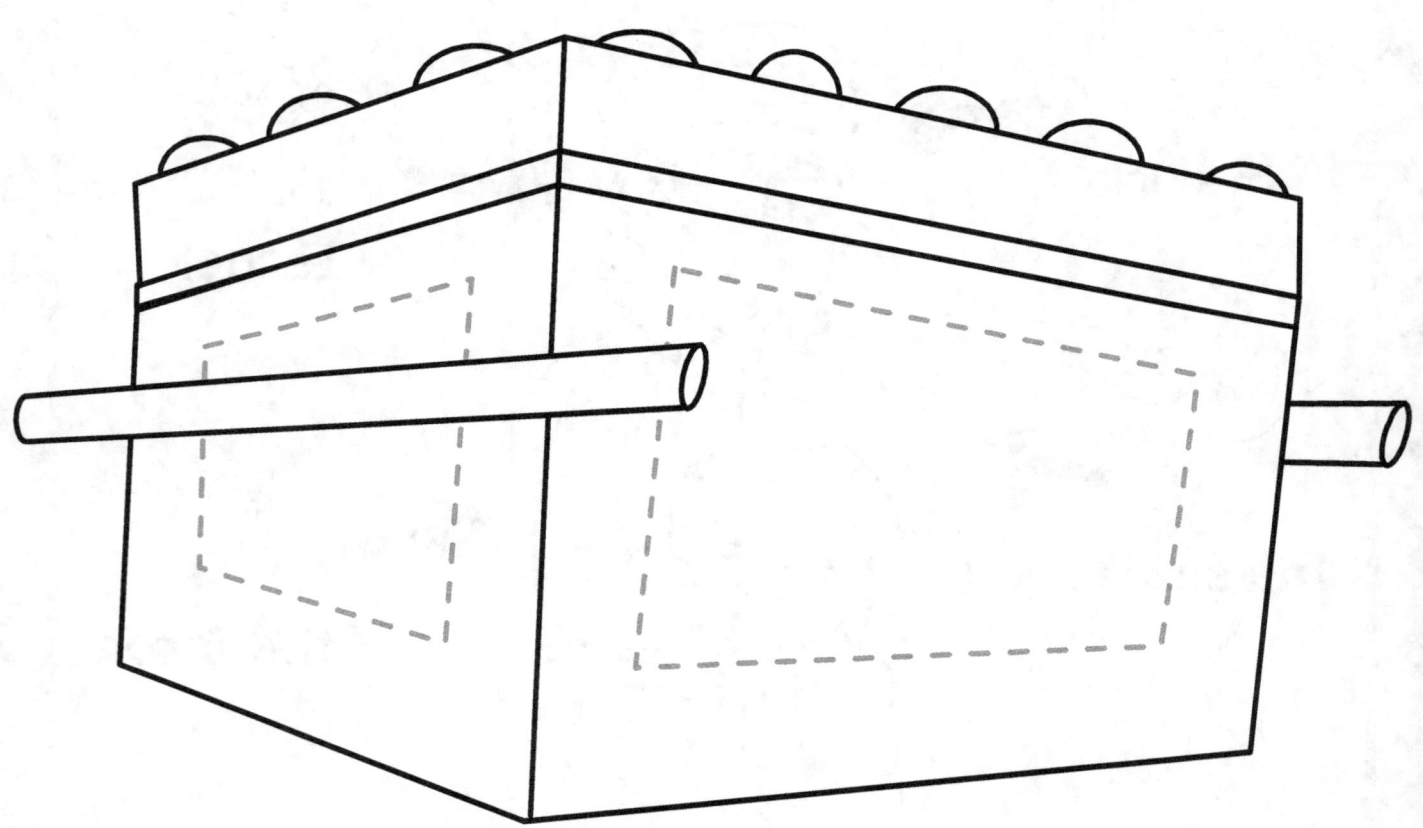

The Israelites' journey

The Israelites left Egypt and headed to the land of Canaan (the Promised Land). Connect the dots to see their journey from Egypt to the Jordan River.

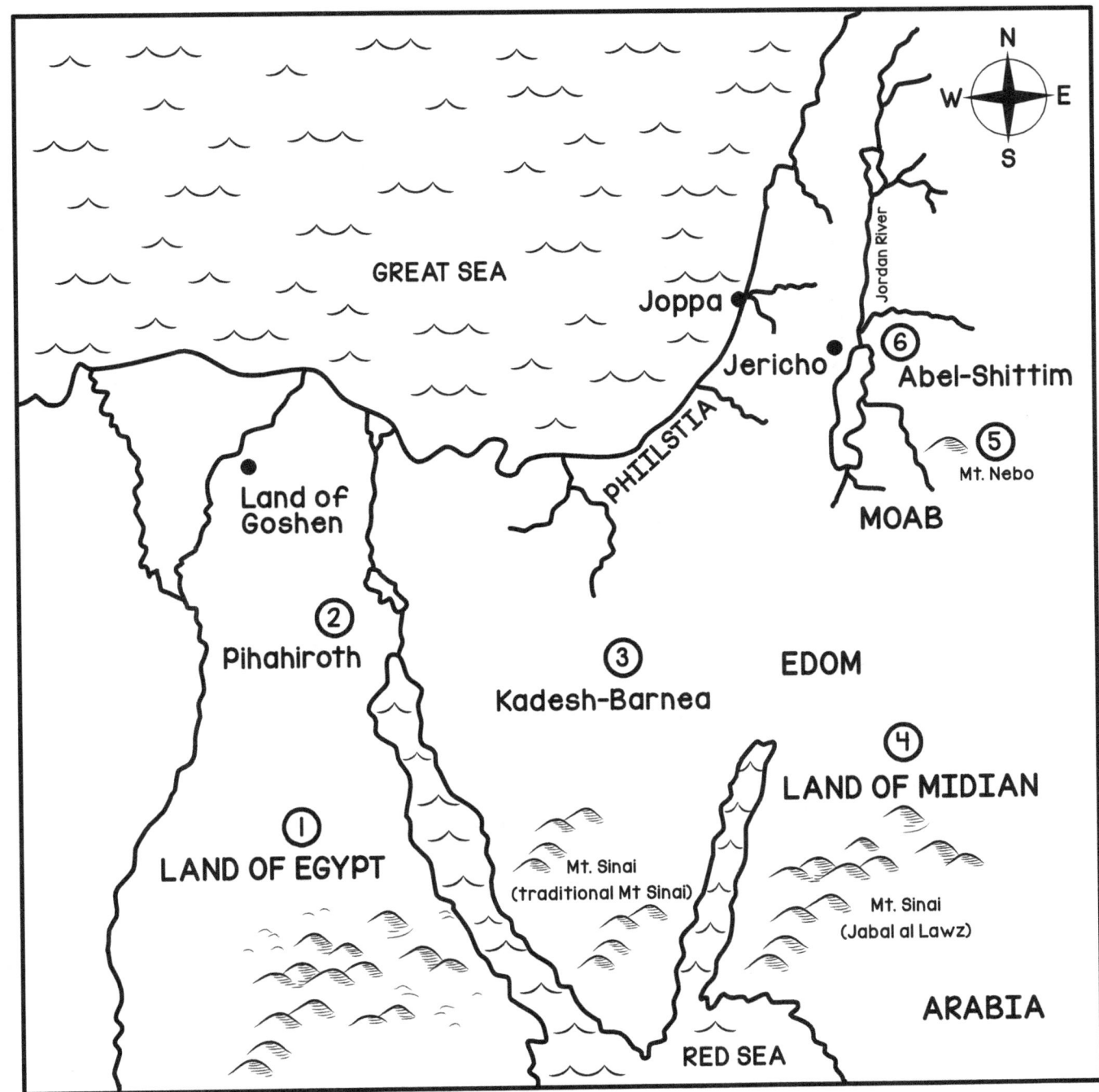

Spies into Canaan

Moses sent 12 spies to see the land of Canaan;
one spy from each tribe of Israel.
What did they find? (Numbers 13:1, 26-29).
Trace the words. Color the pictures.

Big fruit

Big cities

Big people

Who spied out Canaan?

Yah told Moses to choose one man from each tribe of Israel to spy out the land of Canaan (Numbers 13:1-2). Can you count to 12? Count the boxes and write the correct number in an empty box below.

1			**4**
Shammua	Shaphat	Caleb	Igal
	6		
Hoshea	Palti	Gaddiel	Gaddi
9			**12**
Ammiel	Sethur	Nahbi	Geuel

🌿 Korah rebels 🌿

Some men from the tribe of Levi complained about Moses and Aaron. Yah was not happy! (Numbers 16). What happened to the men and their families?

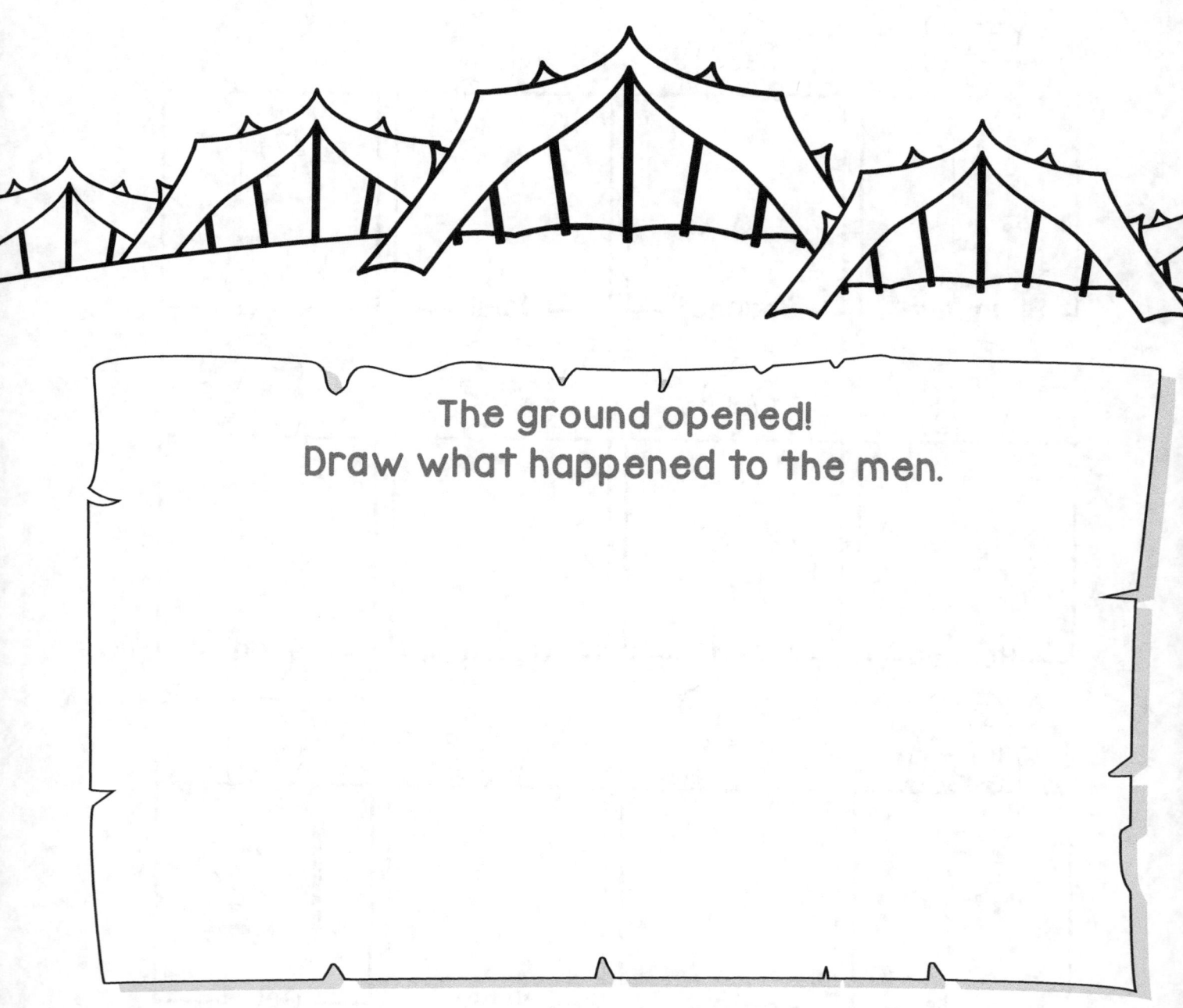

The ground opened!
Draw what happened to the men.

🌿 Aaron is the high priest 🌿

How did Yah show the Israelites that Aaron was the high priest? He made Aaron's staff sprout flowers and almonds (Numbers 17:8). Why did He do this? Write Aaron's name on the staff below. Then, trace and color Aaron's staff.

The talking donkey

King Balak wanted to stop the Israelites from going to the Promised Land. He told Balaam to curse the Israelites. But Yah stopped him with a talking donkey (Numbers 22:28). Name the parts of a donkey.

ear

eye

mouth

tail

leg

🌿 Balaam blesses Israel 🌿

Read Numbers 23:1-2. Balaam told King Balak to build him seven altars. Trace and color the altar below.

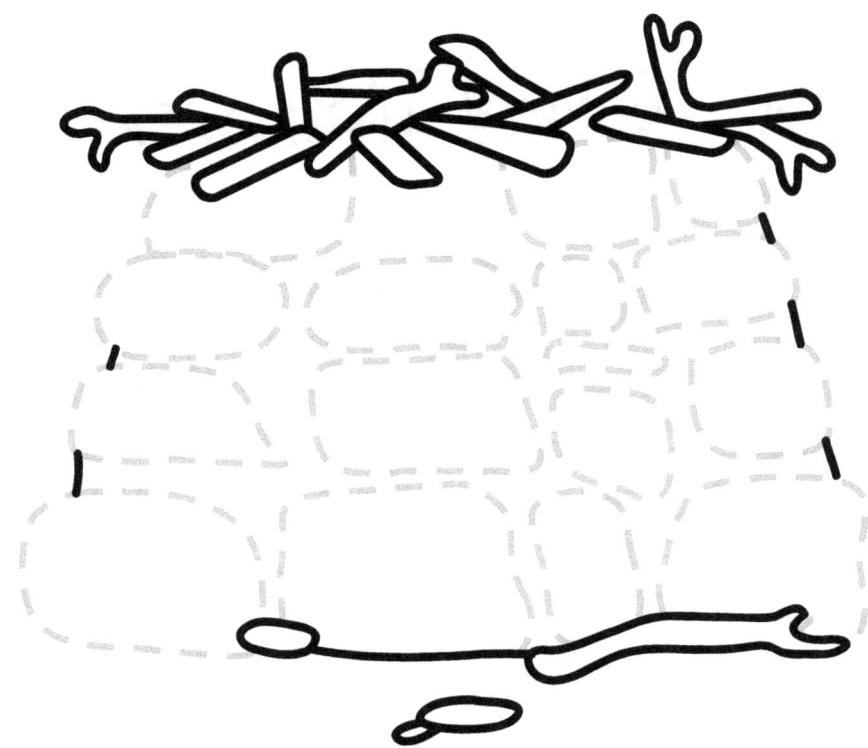

Circle the animals that Balaam put on the altars.

" I am giving you this land. Go and take it. "

(Deuteronomy 1:8)

Did you know?

Circle and color the tabernacle.

Circle and color the sukkah.

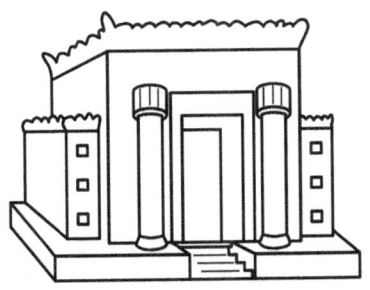  

Circle and color the high priest's breastplate.

Help the spies escape Jericho

The Israelites wanted to destroy Jericho. They sent two men to spy out the city (Joshua 2). The men hid under flax on top of Rahab's house. Draw some flax on the roof. Glue a piece of red string from the window to help the spies escape the city.

🌿 The priests' feet 🌿

The Israelites were ready to cross the Jordan River.
The priests went ahead, carrying the ark of the covenant.
When they stepped in the water, the water stopped!

You will need:
1. Cardboard
2. Marker
3. Scissors
4. Pipe cleaners

Instructions:

1. Draw a large foot onto a piece of cardboard and cut it out.
2. Turn it over and trace onto another piece of cardboard, and cut out. This way you will get a matching left and right foot.
3. Cut four holes into each foot around where your child's foot will go. Thread the pipe cleaners through from the back (two pipe cleaners for each foot). Place your child's feet onto the cardboard feet and fasten with the pipe cleaners.

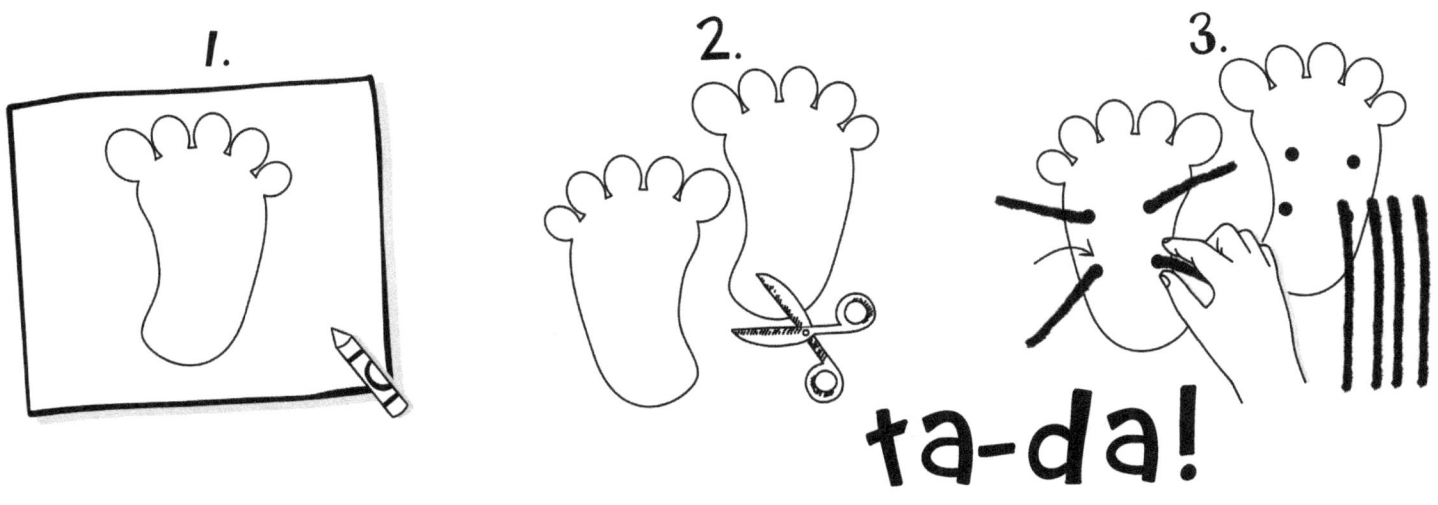

ta-da!

YOU NEED A REMINDER!

After the Israelites crossed the Jordan River, they put 12 rocks at the place where they camped; one rock for each tribe of Israel. The rocks reminded the Israelites what Yah had done. Trace and color each rock a different color. Can you name the tribes?

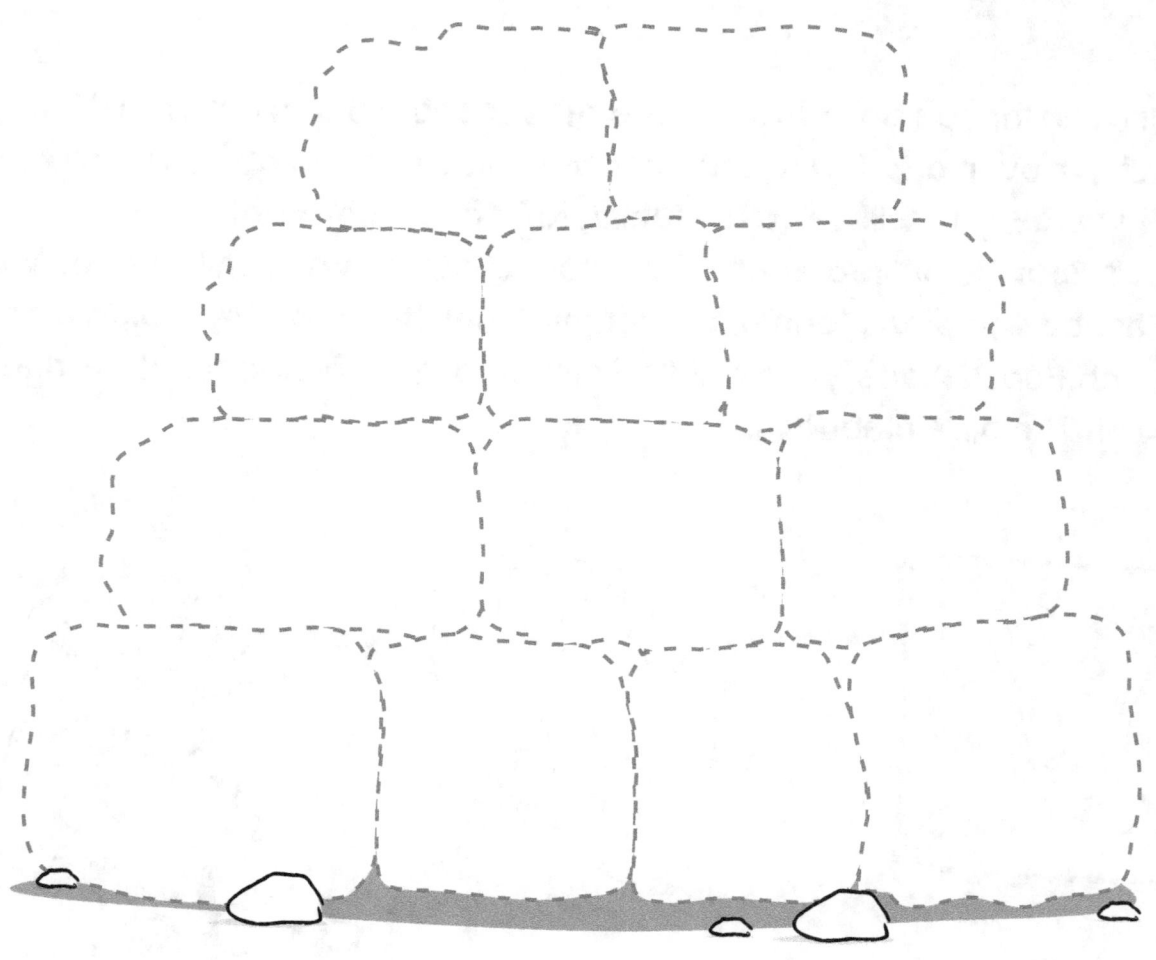

Wilderness menu

Read Joshua 5:10-12. The day after the Passover, God stopped giving the people manna to eat. Instead they ate food from the land of Canaan. Draw an Israelite meal on the plate below.

Circle the food that the Israelites ate in the land of Canaan.

Make a shofar

The Israelites were ready for battle. Joshua told the priests to march around the city of Jericho and blow the shofars.

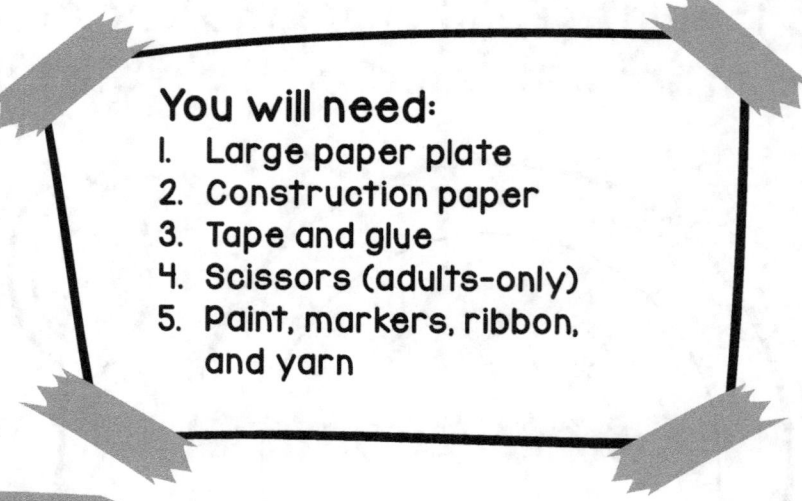

You will need:
1. Large paper plate
2. Construction paper
3. Tape and glue
4. Scissors (adults-only)
5. Paint, markers, ribbon, and yarn

Instructions:

1. Roll a large paper plate into a cone shape. Fasten with tape.
2. Glue construction paper around the cone shape. Use markers, ribbon or paint to decorate your 'shofar'.
3. Thread a piece of yarn through the inside of your shofar. Tie the ends to make a handle.

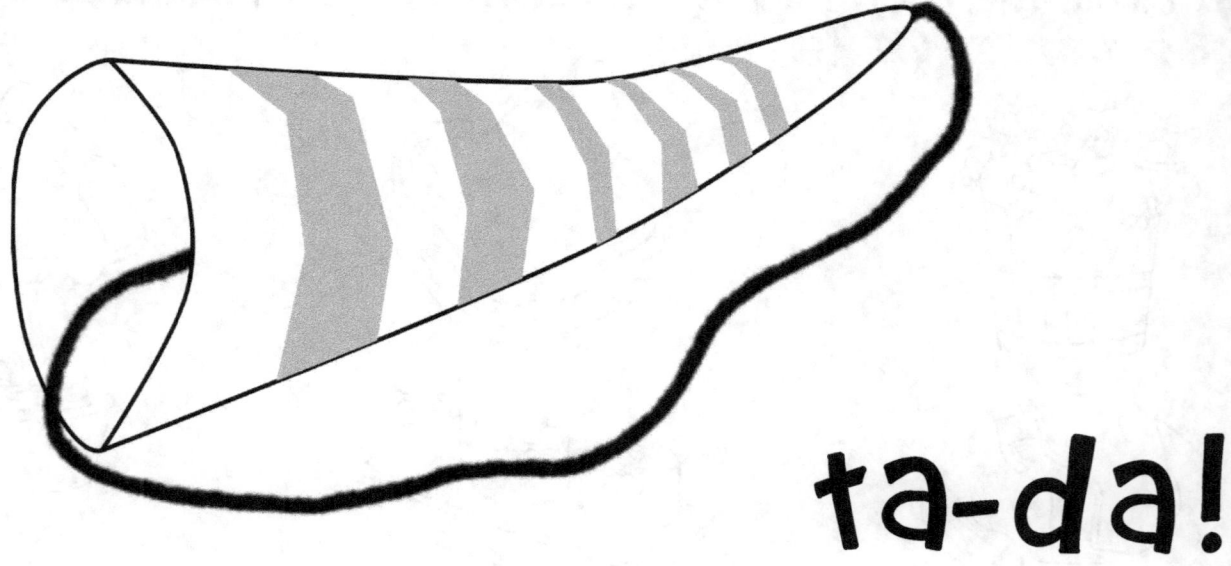

ta-da!

A shofar!

A shofar is made from a ram's horn.
Connect the dots to see the picture.

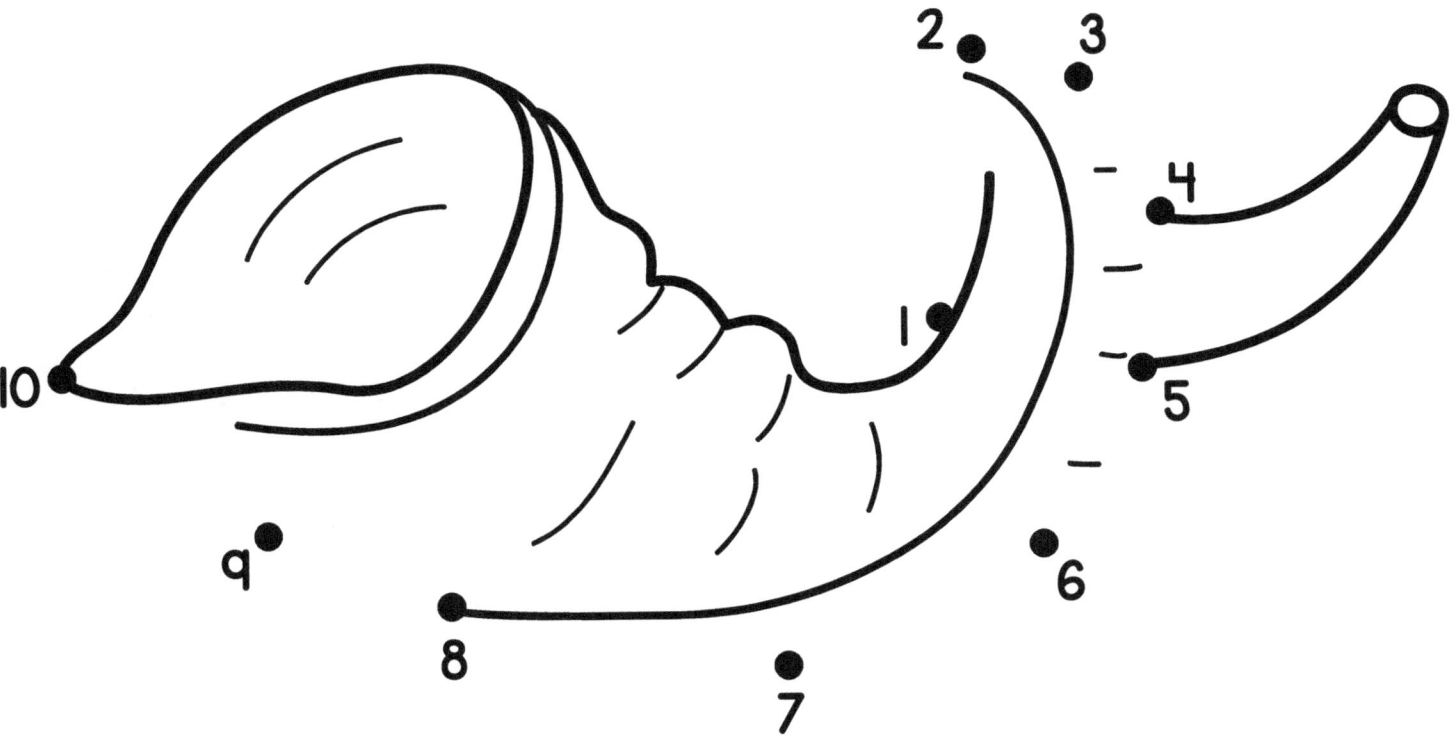

🌿 Walls of Jericho 🌿

The Israelites won the battle (Joshua 6)! Give each child a city wall template and pieces of colored paper. Paste the paper to build the walls of Jericho. On the next worksheet, ask them to draw what Jericho looked like after the walls fell down.

" Be Strong and of a good Courage. "

(Joshua 1:9)

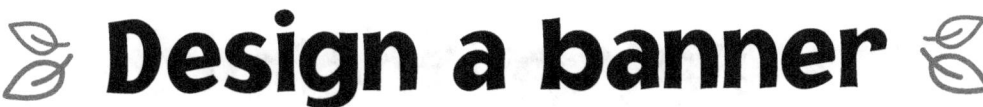 Design a banner

Each tribe of Israel had its own standard
(Numbers 1:52). A standard is a type of banner.
Design and color your own banner.

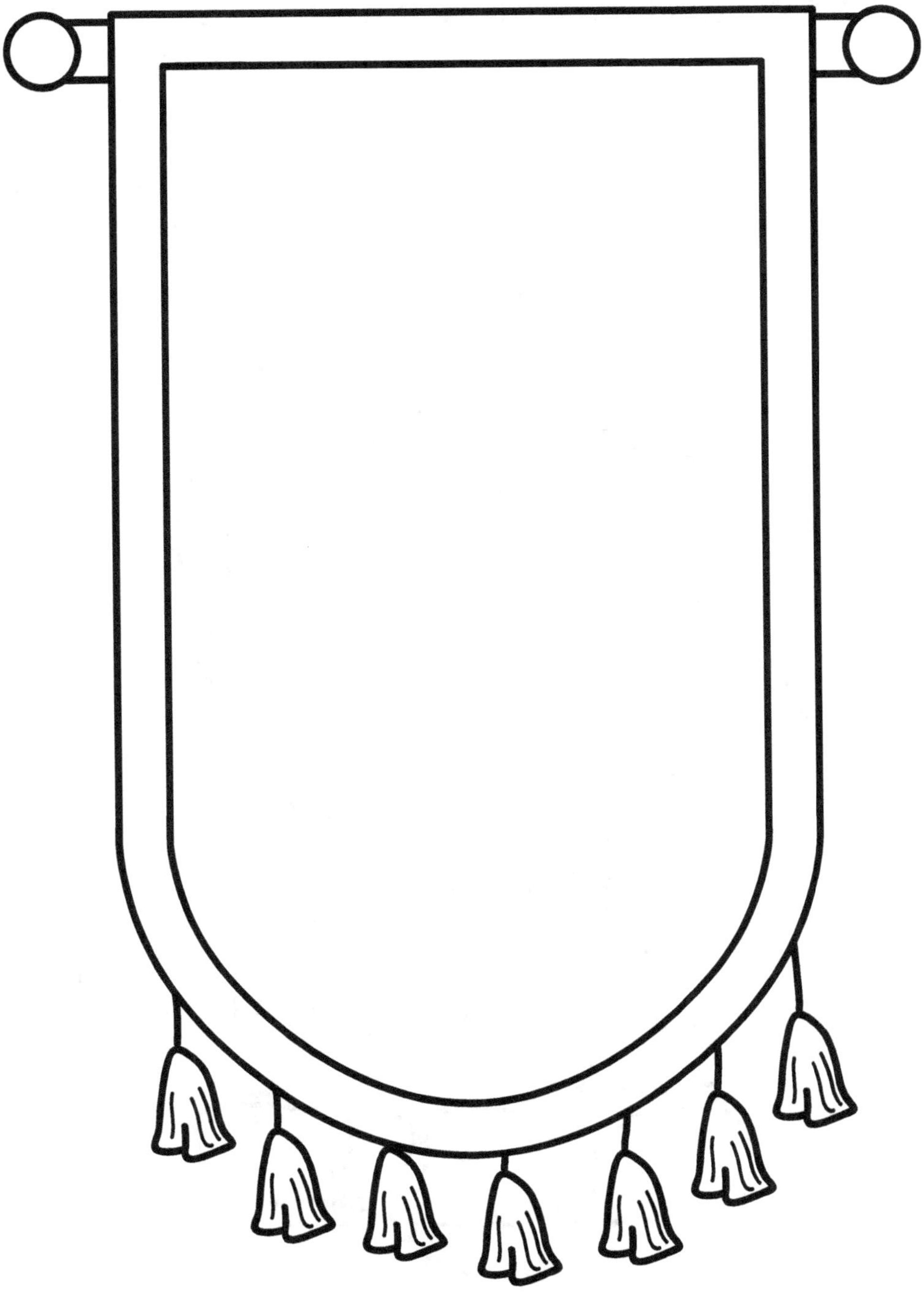

🌿 False gods 🌿

Yah wanted the Israelites to only worship Him.
He told them to burn people's false gods
(Deuteronomy 7:25). Trace a dotted line from
each object to the fire. Color the pictures.

Battle of Ai

The Israelites set fire to the city of Ai.
They won the battle (Joshua 8).
Draw smoke and fire to complete the picture.

Follow the path to Canaan

Help the Israelites make their way to the
Promised Land by following the path from A to Z.

The promised land

In the land of Canaan, each tribe was given a piece of land.
Use the color code to finish the map.

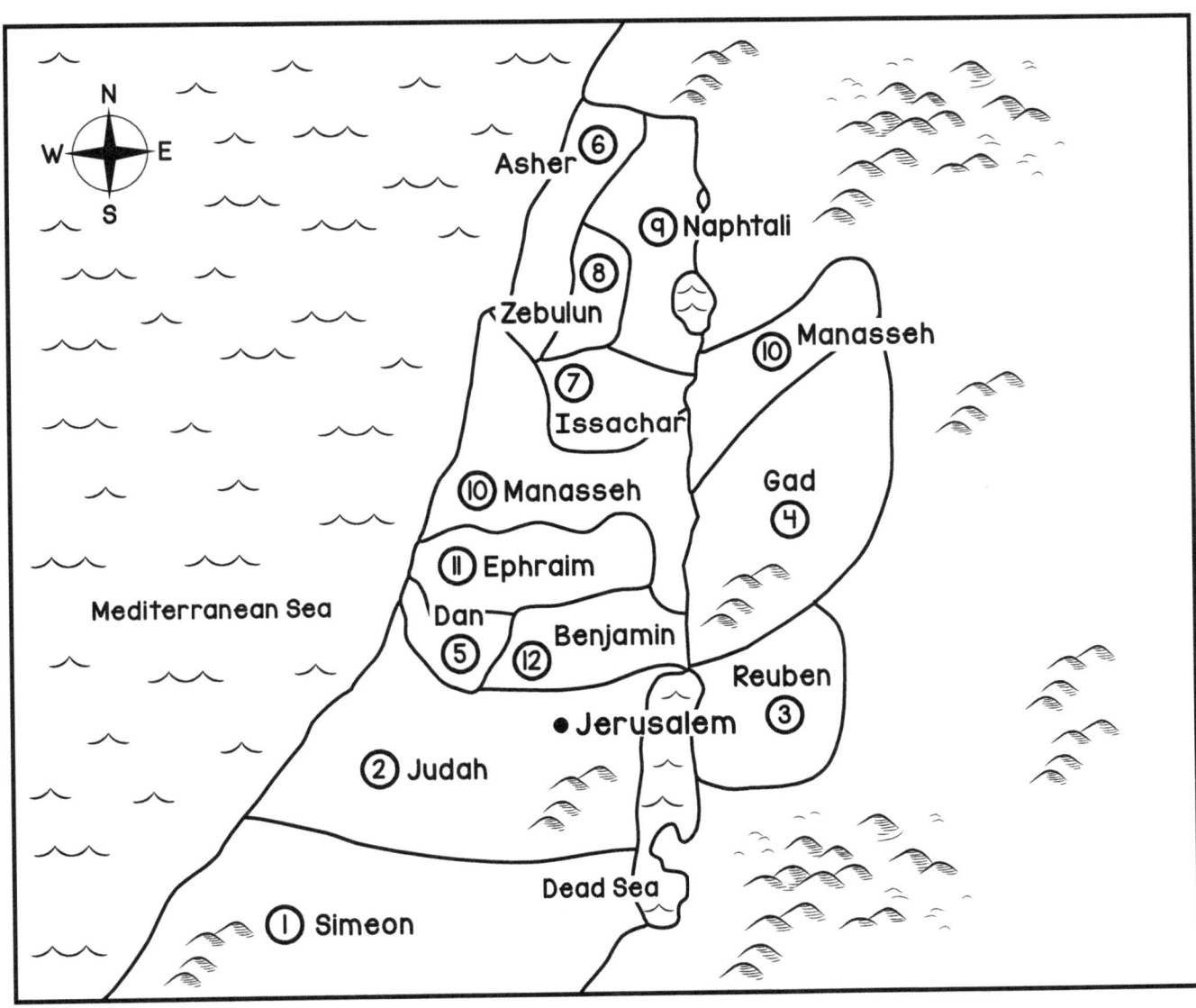

1 = green (Simeon)

2 = purple (Judah)

3 = orange (Reuben)

4 = grey (Gad)

5 = blue (Dan)

6 = yellow (Asher)

7 = light blue (Issachar)

8 = white (Zebulun)

9 = pink (Naphtali)

10 = light green (Manasseh)

11 = black (Ephraim)

12 = brown (Benjamin)

Let's learn Hebrew

The sons and grandsons
of Jacob (Israel)

✴ Re'uven ✴

The Hebrew name for Reuben is Re'uven.
Reuben was the 1st son of Jacob (Israel). Reuben
stopped his brothers killing Joseph (Genesis 37).

Re'uven

רְאוּבֵן

Reuben

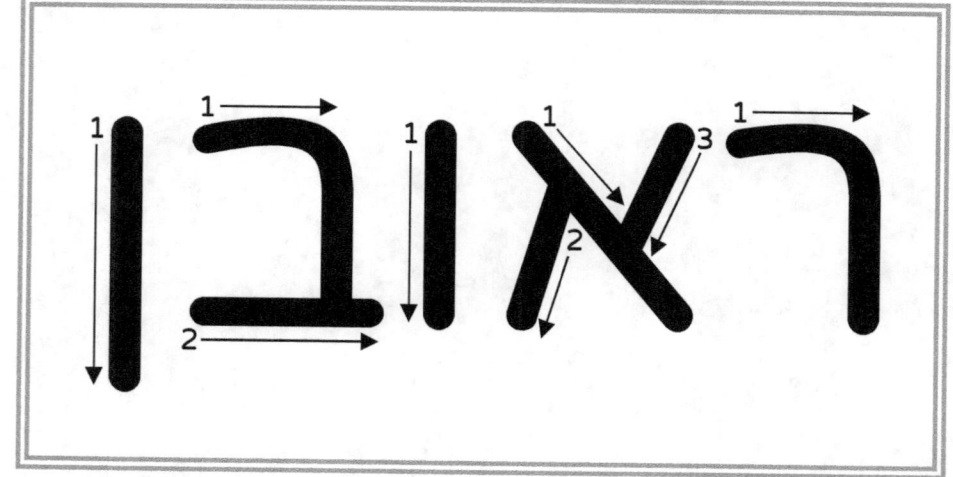

 # Let's write!

Practice writing Reuben's Hebrew
name on the lines below.

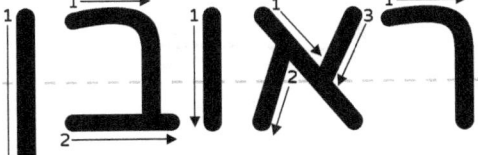

Try this on your own.
Remember that Hebrew is read from RIGHT to LEFT.

✦ Shim'on ✦

The Hebrew name for Simeon is Shim'on. Simeon was the 2nd son of Jacob (Israel). When Jacob's sons went to Egypt to buy food, Joseph put Simeon in prison (Genesis 42-43).

Shim'on

שִׁמְעוֹן

Simeon

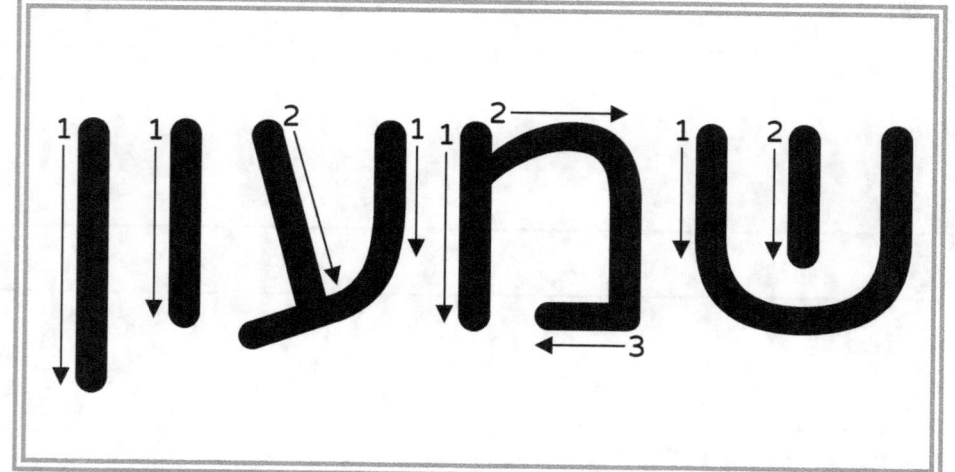

Bible Pathway Adventures

Let's write!

Practice writing Simeon's Hebrew
name on the lines below.

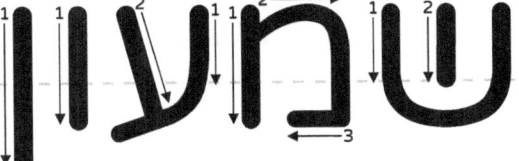

שמעון

Try this on your own.
Remember that Hebrew is read from RIGHT to LEFT.

✦ Levi ✦

The Hebrew name for Levi is Levi. Levi was the 3rd son of Jacob (Israel). Priests were chosen from the tribe of Levi. They took care of the tabernacle and taught the Torah.

Levi

לֵוִי

Levi

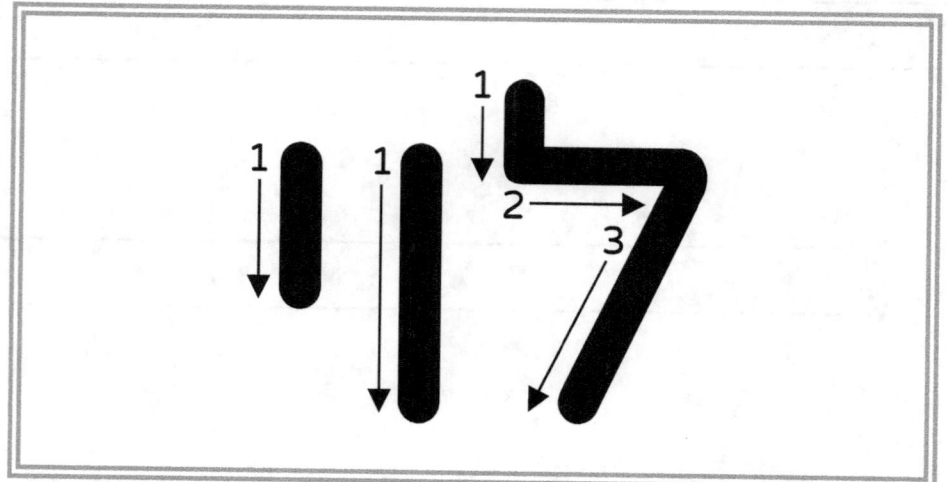

Let's write!

Practice writing Levi's Hebrew
name on the lines below.

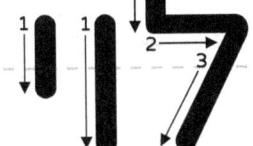

Try this on your own.
Remember that Hebrew is read from RIGHT to LEFT.

✸ Yehudah ✸

The Hebrew name for Judah is Yehudah. Judah was the 4th son of Jacob (Israel). Judah told his brothers to sell Joseph to the slave traders. Yeshua is of the tribe of Judah.

Yehudah

יְהוּדָה

Judah

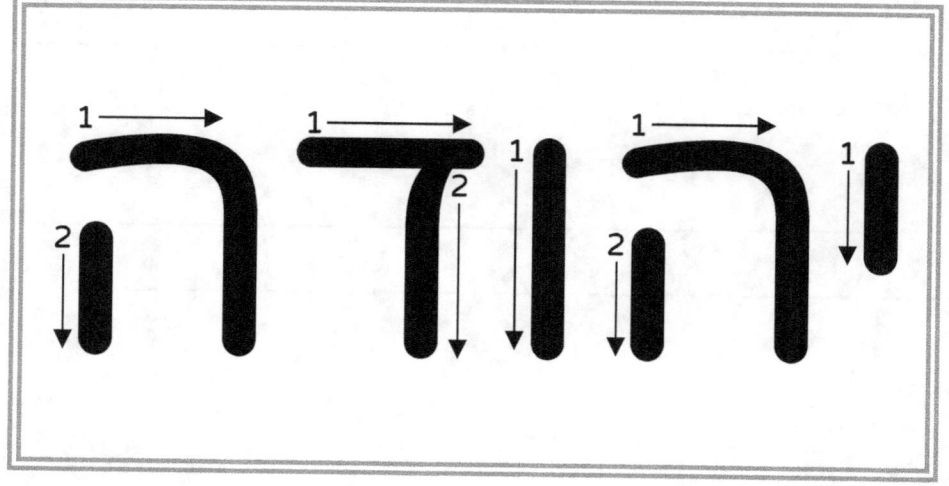

 # Let's write!

Practice writing Judah's Hebrew name on the lines below.

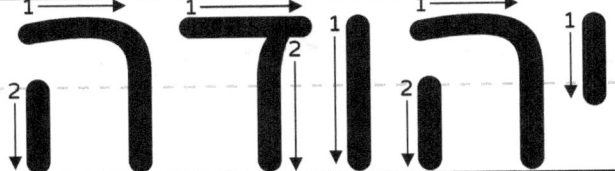

Try this on your own.
Remember that Hebrew is read from RIGHT to LEFT.

✶ Dan ✶

The Hebrew name for Dan is Dan.
Dan was the 5th son of Jacob (Israel).
Samson was of the tribe of Dan (Judges 13:2).

Dan

דָן

Dan

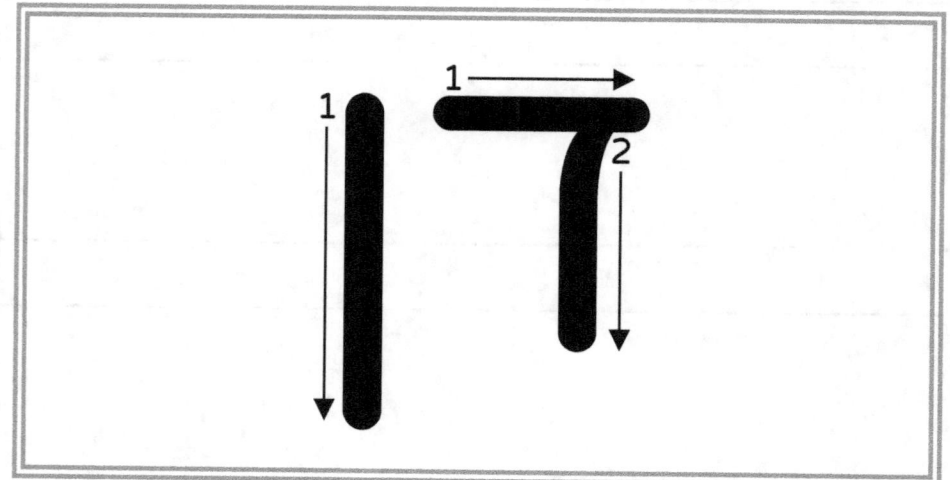

 # Let's write!

Practice writing Dan's Hebrew
name on the lines below.

דן

דן

Try this on your own.
Remember that Hebrew is read from RIGHT to LEFT.

✦ Naftali ✦

The Hebrew name for Naphtali is Naftali. Naphtali was the 6th son of Jacob (Israel). The tribe of Naphtali helped Gideon and David fight their enemies.

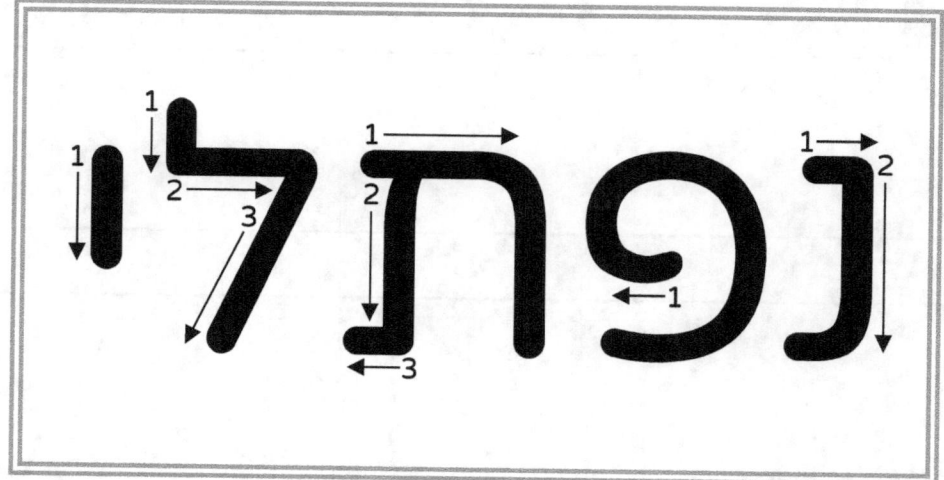

Naftali

נַפְתָּלִי

Naphtali

 # Let's write!

Practice writing Naphtali's Hebrew
name on the lines below.

נפתלי

נפתלי

Try this on your own.
Remember that Hebrew is read from RIGHT to LEFT.

✷ Gad ✷

The Hebrew name for Gad is Gad. Gad was the 7th son of Jacob (Israel). Men from the tribe of Gad were brave warriors, always ready for battle.

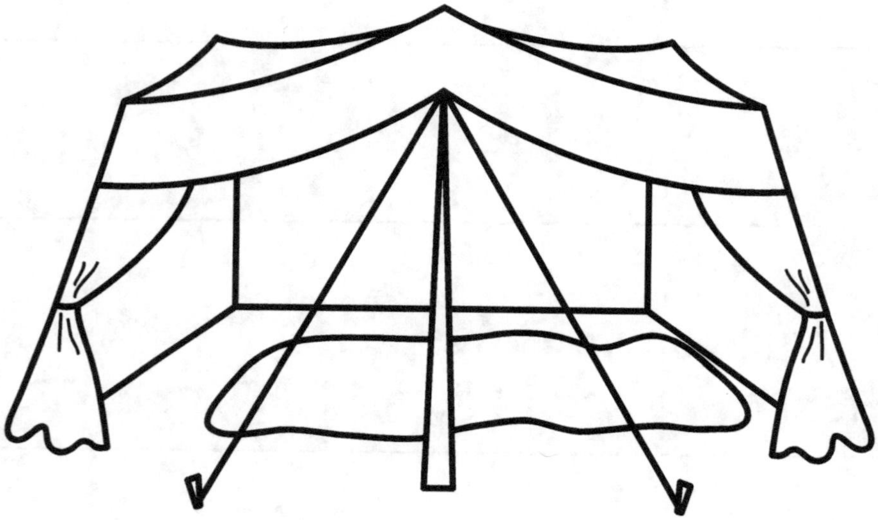

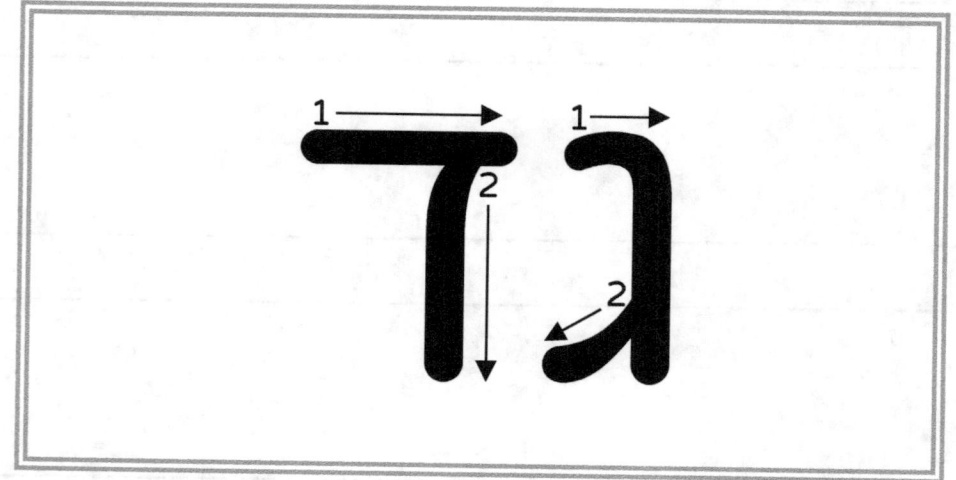

Gad

גָּד

Gad

 # Let's write!

Practice writing Gad's Hebrew
name on the lines below.

גד

גד

Try this on your own.
Remember that Hebrew is read from RIGHT to LEFT.

⭐ Asher ⭐

The Hebrew name for Asher is Asher.
Asher was the 8th son of Jacob (Israel).
The tribe of Asher grew olives and made lots of olive oil.

Asher

אָשֵׁר

Asher

 # Let's write!

Practice writing Asher's Hebrew
name on the lines below.

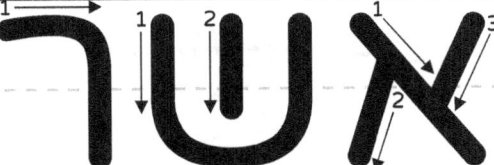

Try this on your own.
Remember that Hebrew is read from RIGHT to LEFT.

✴ Yisachar ✴

The Hebrew name for Issachar is Yisachar.
Issachar was the 9th son of Jacob (Israel).
The tribe of Issachar liked to study the Torah.

Yisachar

יִשָּׂשכָר

Issachar

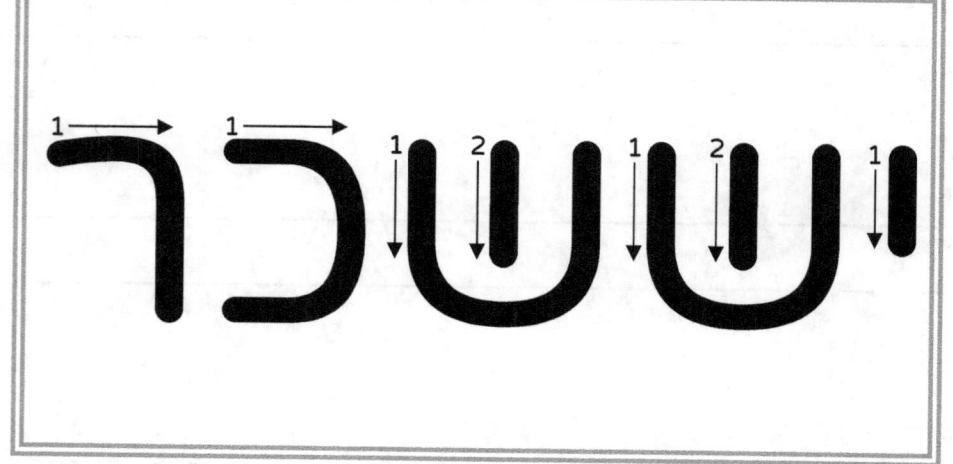

 # Let's write!

Practice writing Issachar's Hebrew
name on the lines below.

יששכר

יששכר

Try this on your own.
Remember that Hebrew is read from RIGHT to LEFT.

✶ Zevulun ✶

The Hebrew name for Zebulun is Zevulun. Zebulun was the 10th son of Jacob (Israel). Jacob blessed Zebulun, saying, "You will live by the sea and be a safe place for ships."

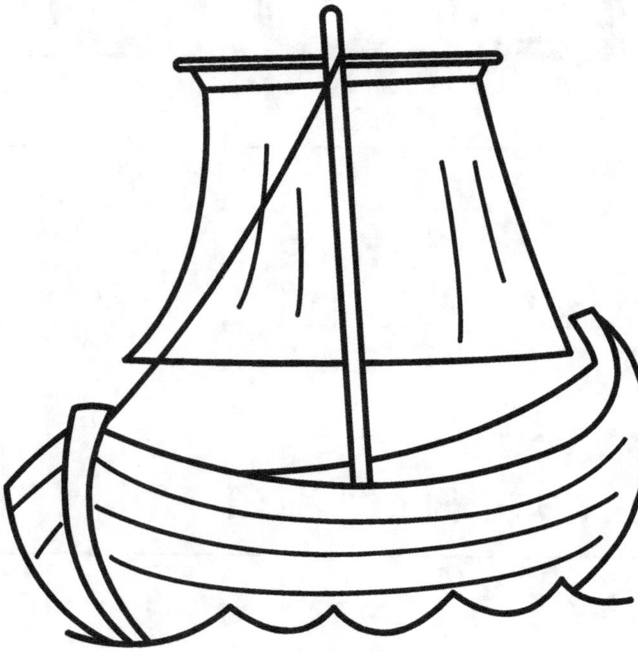

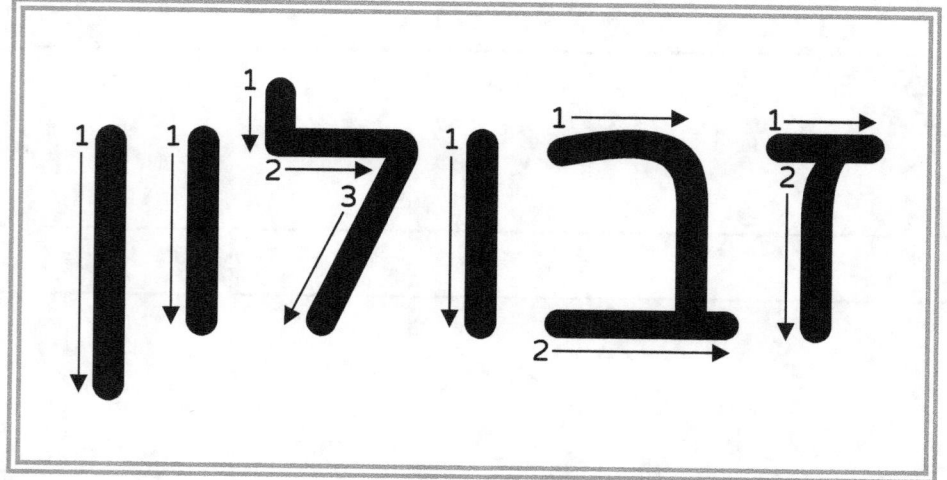

Zevulun

זְבוּלוּן

Zebulun

 # Let's write!

Practice writing Zebulun's Hebrew
name on the lines below.

זבולון

זבולון

Try this on your own.
Remember that Hebrew is read from RIGHT to LEFT.

✦ Yosef ✦

The Hebrew name for Joseph is Yosef. Joseph was the 11th son of Jacob (Israel). His brothers sold him as a slave. But later, he helped rule the land of Egypt.

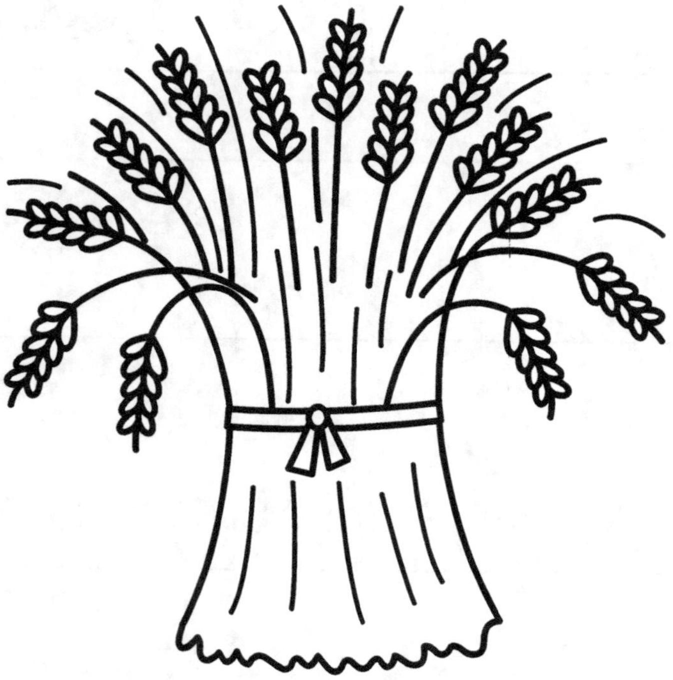

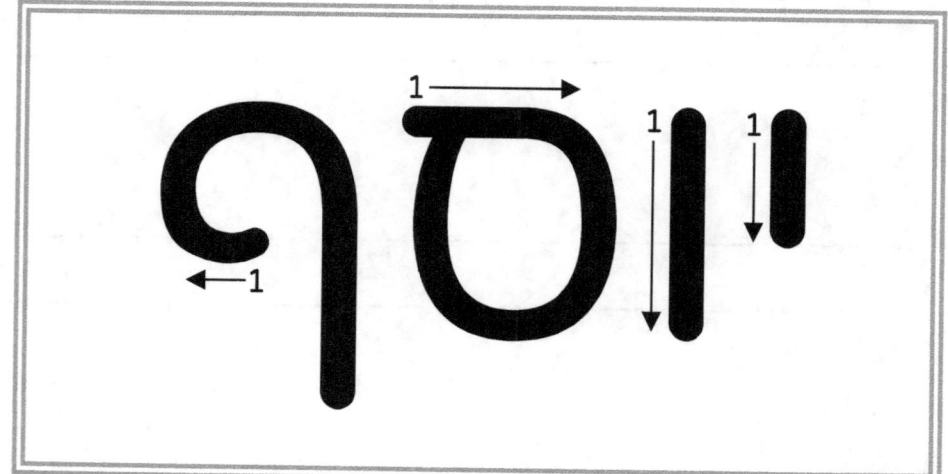

Yosef

יוֹסֵף

Joseph

 # Let's write!

Practice writing Joseph's Hebrew
name on the lines below.

יוֹסֵף

יוֹסֵף

Try this on your own.
Remember that Hebrew is read from RIGHT to LEFT.

✦ Binyamin ✦

The Hebrew name for Benjamin is Binyamin. Benjamin was the 12th son of Jacob (Israel). The tribe of Benjamin were good fighters. They used bows and arrows to win battles.

Binyamin

בִּנְיָמִין

Benjamin

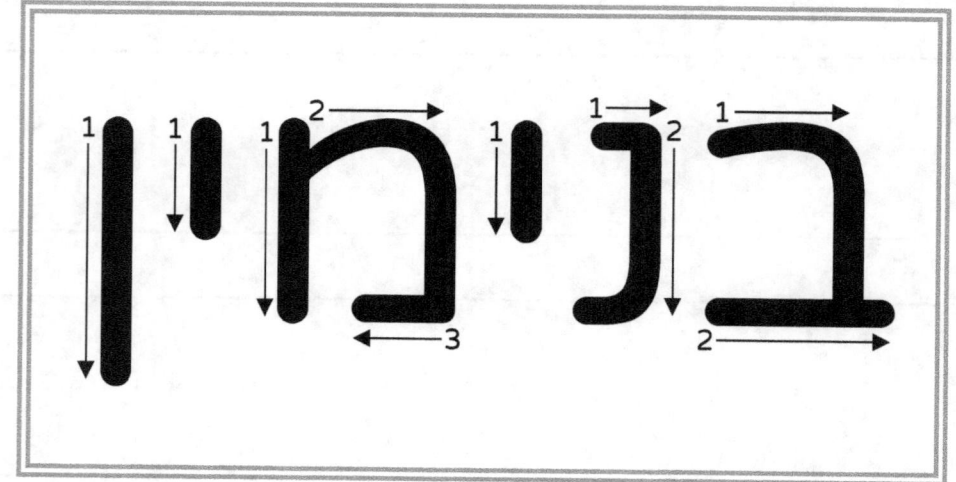

 # Let's write!

Practice writing Benjamin's Hebrew
name on the lines below.

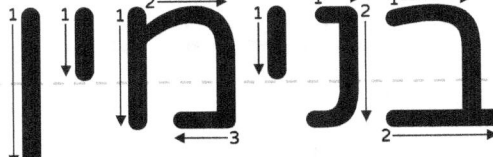

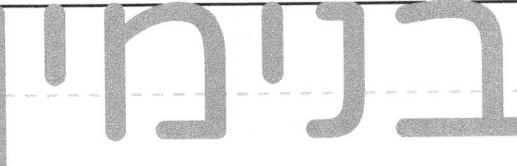

Try this on your own.
Remember that Hebrew is read from RIGHT to LEFT.

✸ Menasheh ✸

The Hebrew name for Manasseh is Menasheh. Manasseh was a son of Joseph, and the grandson of Jacob (Israel). Gideon was of the tribe of Manasseh (Judges 6:15).

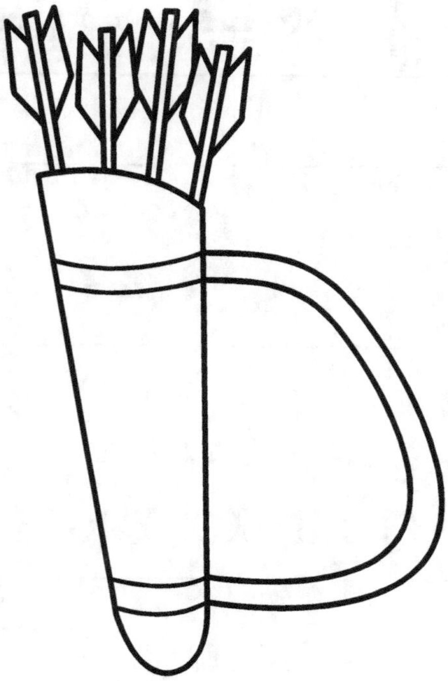

Menasheh

מְנַשֶּׁה

Manasseh

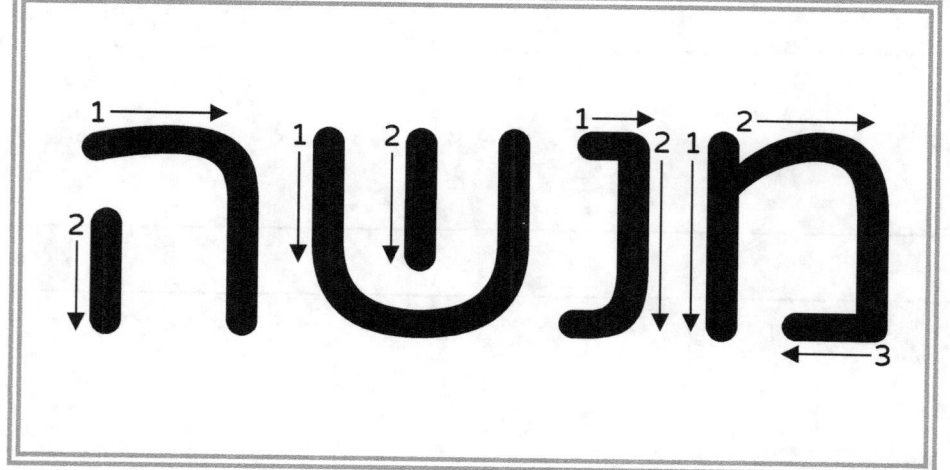

 # Let's write!

Practice writing Manasseh's Hebrew
name on the lines below.

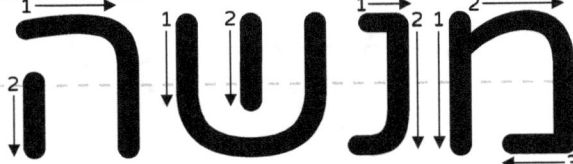

מנשה

Try this on your own.
Remember that Hebrew is read from RIGHT to LEFT.

✦ Efrayim ✦

The Hebrew name for Ephraim is Efrayim. Ephraim was a son of Joseph, and the grandson of Jacob (Israel). Joshua was of the tribe of Ephraim.

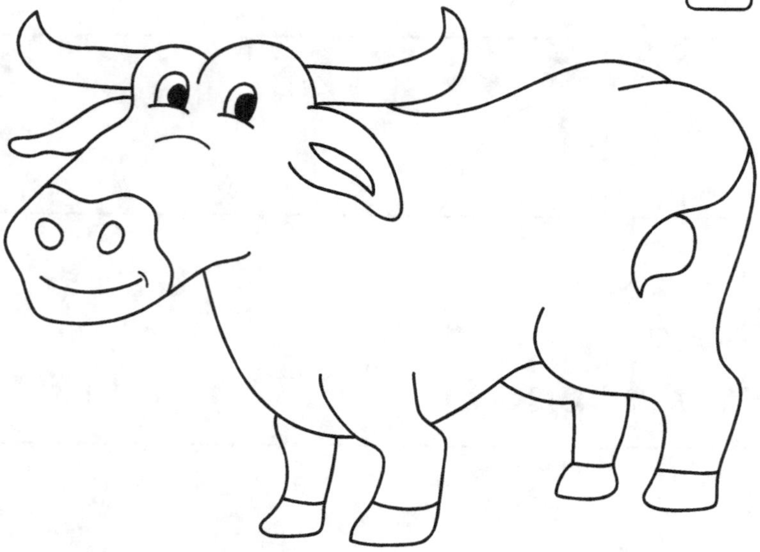

Efrayim

אֶפְרַיִם

Ephraim

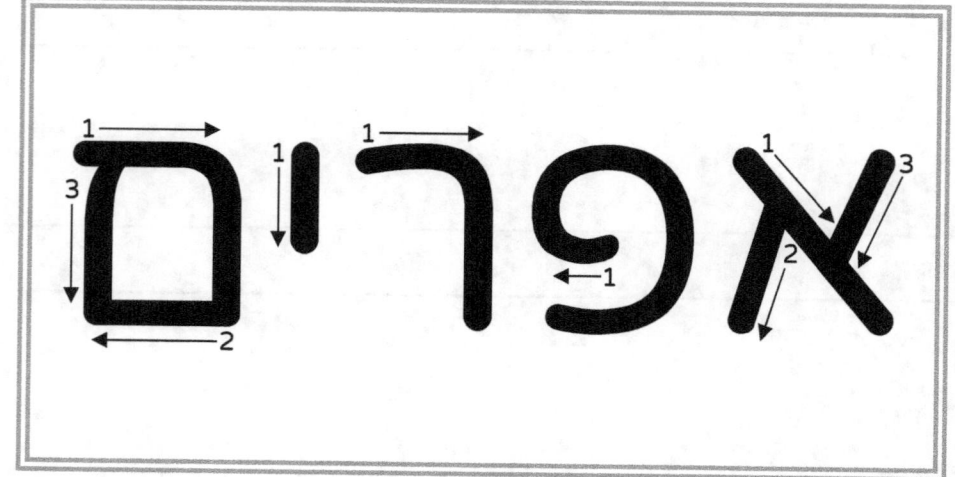

Adventures

 # Let's write!

Practice writing Ephraim's Hebrew
name on the lines below.

אפרים

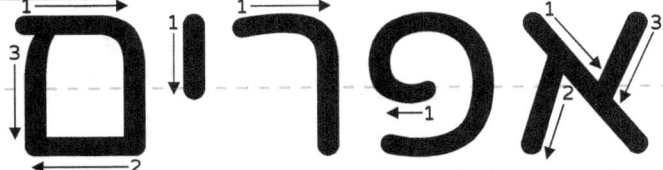

Try this on your own.
Remember that Hebrew is read from RIGHT to LEFT.

Flashcards

The sons and grandsons of Jacob (Israel)

Color and cut out the flashcards.
Tape them around your home or classroom.

ראובן

Re'uven / Reuben

1

שמעון

Shim'On / Simeon

2

יהודה

Yehudah / Judah

3

יששכר

Yisachar / Issachar

4

✂

דן

Dan / Dan

5

נפתלי

Naftali / Naphtali

6

גד

Gad / Gad

7

אשר

Asher / Asher

8

✂

זבולון

Zevulun / Zebulun
ק

בנימין

Binyamin / Benjamin
10

מנשה

Menasheh / Manasseh
11

אפרים

Efrayim / Ephraim
12

יוסף

Yosef / Joseph

13

לוי

Levi / Levi

14

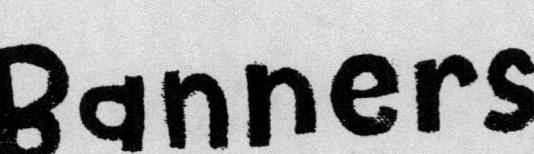

Banners

Twelve tribes of Israel
(Numbers 1:1-42)

REUBEN

SIMEON

JUDAH

DAN

NAPHTALI

GAD

ASHER

ISSACHAR

ZEBULUN

BENJAMIN

MANASSEH

EPHRAIM

Crafts & Projects

Ten Plagues of Egypt

Print and color the ten plagues of Egypt.
Cut out each plague and paste it onto a wooden stick.

Israelites make a Golden Calf

Aaron made a calf out of gold for the Israelites
to worship. Yah was not pleased! (Exodus 32)
Color and cut out the people. Place them around the calf.

Aaron

Israelite

Israelite

🌿 The tabernacle 🌿

The Israelites made special furniture for the tabernacle.
Cut out the furniture and place them in the tabernacle.

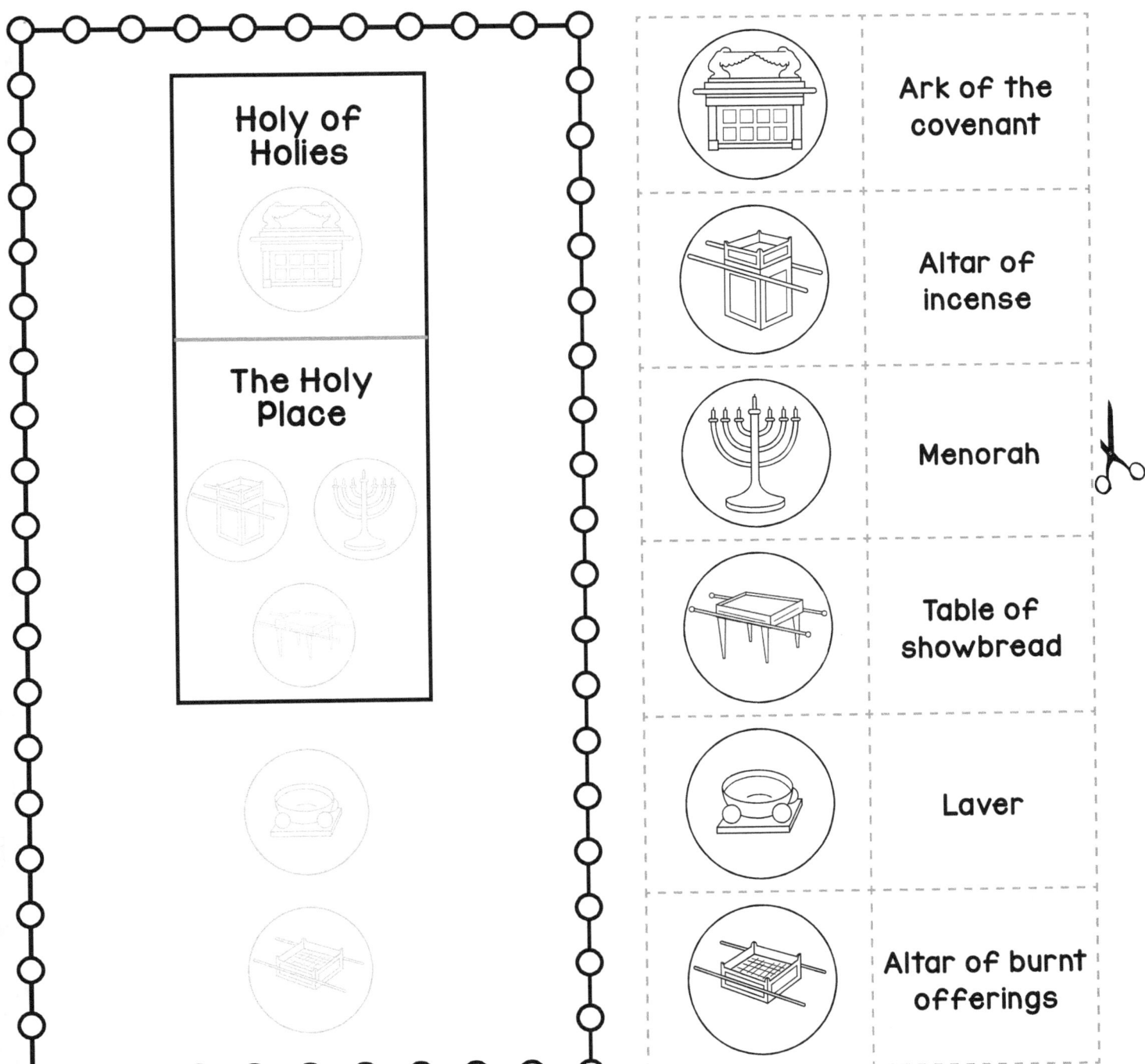

Holy of Holies

The Holy Place

Ark of the covenant

Altar of incense

Menorah

Table of showbread

Laver

Altar of burnt offerings

Let's make a menorah!

The Israelites made a golden menorah (lampstand) to put inside the tabernacle. Color and cut out your menorah and candles. Tape the candles to the menorah.

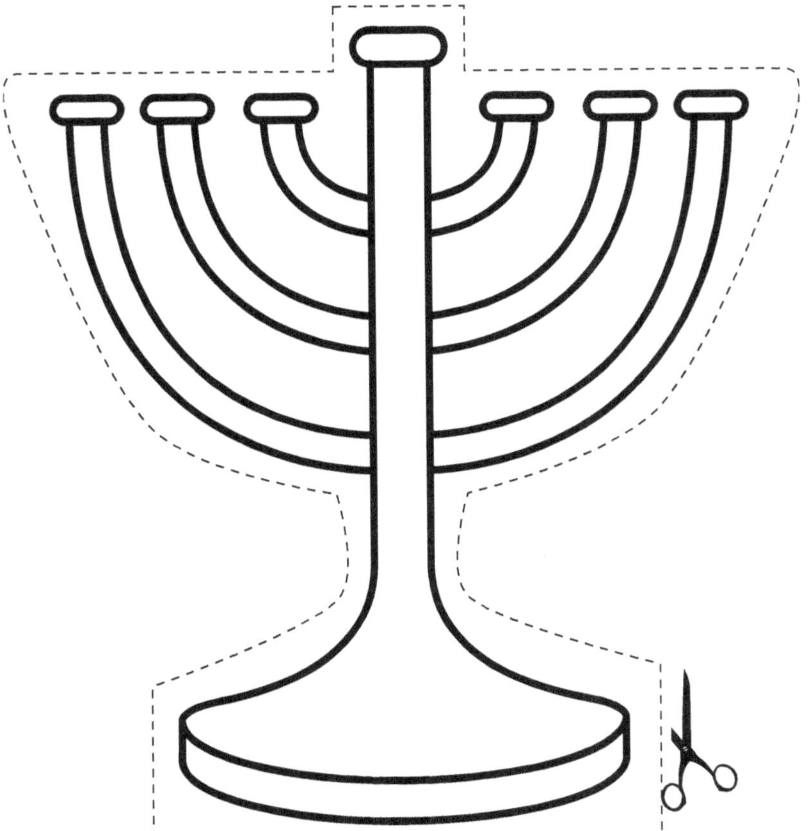

Discover more Activity Books!

Available for purchase at shop.biblepathwayadventures.com

www.ingramcontent.com/pod-product-compliance
Lightning Source LLC
Chambersburg PA
CBHW081330120626
46546CB00011B/3289